To free oneself of knowledge is to die, and thus one lives.

Krishnamurti

Danielle and Olivier Föllmi

WISDOM

365 THOUGHTS FROM INDIAN MASTERS

with the collaboration of Muthusamy Varadarajan
Foreword by Giuliano Boccali
Introduction by Jean Sellier
Captions by Radhika Jha

Mata Amritanandamayi—The Bhagavad Gita—Buddha—Chandralekha—Mahatma Gandhi
Ramchandra Gandhi—His Holiness the XIVth Dalai Lama—Kabir—Kalidasa—Krishnamurti
Acharya Mahaprajna—Sri Ramana Maharshi—Mira Bai—Guru Nanak—Patanjali—Svami Prajnanpad
Maa Purnananda—Rev. Parthasarathi Rajagopalachari—Gopal Singh—Rabindranath Tagore
The Upanishads—Valluvar—The Vedas—Swami Vivekananda

Harry N. Abrams, Inc., Publishers
New York

Foreword

Its natural landscape encompasses all that can be offered the world over: endless snow, breathtaking peaks, the desert, luxurious virgin forests, plains furrowed with wide rivers, colors and perfumes from the strongest to the most delicate. In the same way, its culture is an inexhaustible reservoir; a treasure trove, we could say, of all that humanity can offer us. Its incomparable diversity without doubt comes from the fact that India for over three thousand years has never rejected nor eliminated any part of its history or endeavors. It is at once a land of the silence of meditation and the voice of prayer, a land of a logic most subtle and the spell of sensuality, a land of fervent passions and calm equanimity. Its melody is that of a thousand words and songs, whether from village huts under serene night skies or from the incessant hustle and bustle of the megalopolis. No wonder, then, that in its myths, concepts of good and evil are not always easily distinguished from one another. In both philosophy and life, illusion and its manifestation merge into a fantasmagoric play, like an image and its evanescent reflection.

Here as nowhere else, both intense emotion and a philosophical detachment can transform everyday reality: the rhythmic movements of artisans, their skill handed down through generations; the bustle of the baths and the pungent aromas of its cuisine; the innocent smiles of the elderly and children; or—and why not?—the energetic activity of the computer programmer. Wisdom, or better, the many wisdoms of India, thus offer a unique itinerary that traces the unforgettable thoughts and images of this book. An itinerary is born from nature with its infinite forms, or of the diverse aspects of ethnic groups, of peoples, of women and men so different, and ends in the profound dimensions of the spirit, which, through numerous forms, invokes the divine down to the unique, total, and eternal face of Humanity.

Giuliano Boccali

Introduction

Coming from Central Asia (most likely Iran), the Aryans entered present-day India about 3,500 years ago, bringing with them their religion, Vedantism. Over time, their culture was infused with the local traditions, while their religion, augmented by complicated rites, became Brahmanism. The desire for a more simple and direct religious spirit subsequently led the Buddha to look for another path, and thus Buddhism was born, about 2,500 years ago. The great majority of Indians, however, have preserved their own traditions, though not without drawing lessons from Buddhism: the subcontinent nurtures Hinduism, but also other Indian, Muslim, and Sikh bodies of wisdom.

Early on, the religious influence and culture of India stretched across the East, into present-day Burma, Thailand, Laos, and Cambodia, as shown in the architecture of the magnificent twelfth-century temple of Angkor, in Cambodia. The Burmese, Thai, and Khmer (Cambodian) languages derive their written form from the Indians. These four countries later adopted Buddhism, which came from India as well, via Ceylon, now Sri Lanka. Indian influence was also felt in Indonesia, before the spread of Islam there in the fourteenth century. Only the Balinese have resisted the tide of Buddhism: they remain, to this day, fervent Hindus.

Jean Sellier

One drop of the sea cannot claim to come from one river, and another drop of the sea from another river; the sea is a single consistent whole. In the same way all beings are one; there is no being that does not come from the soul, and is not part of the soul.

Chandogya Upanishad

A torrent descends from the Himalayas, the home of the gods.

From Him woman was born; and from Her man was born.

From His mind the moon was born; from His eye the sun was born; from His breath the wind was born.

From His navel the atmosphere was born; from His head the sky was born;

and from His ear the four quarters of the sky were born.

Thus the universe was in order.

Rig Veda

The Thar desert in Rajasthan.

He is fire and the sun; he is the moon and the stars, he is the air and the sea.

He is this boy, and that girl. He appears in countless different forms.

He has no beginning, and he has no end. He is the source of all things.

Each type of living being is distinct and different. But when we pierce the veil of difference,

we see the unity of all beings.

Svetasvatara Upanishad

Monsoon season in Tamil Nadu.

In nature, action and reaction are continuous. Everything is connected to everything else.

No one part, nothing, is isolated. Everything is linked, and interdependent.

Everywhere everything is connected to everything else. Each question receives the correct answer.

Svami Prajnanpad

Summer—monsoon clouds against the massifs of the Himalayas.

All humanity shares the sunlight; that sunlight is neither yours nor mine.

It is the life-giving energy, which we all share.

The beauty of a sunset, if you are watching it sensitively, is shared by all human beings.

Krishnamurti

Fresh water feeds the Kerala canals, which line the Arabian Sea.

The energy in the world flows from God at the centre, and back to God.

The sages see life as a wheel, with each individual going round and round through birth and death.

Individuals remain on this wheel so long as they believe themselves to be separate;

but once they realize their unity with God, then they break free.

Svetasvatara Upanishad

The purification ritual in the sacred waters of the Ganges is essential for devout Hindus.
Following pages: Indian choreography representing Unity in Diversity, at dusk in the Kerala.

Unity in diversity is the order of the universe. Just as we are all human, we are all distinct.

As a human being, I am like you. As Mr. X, I am different from you.

As a man, you are different from a woman, but in being all humans, we are one.

In that you are alive, you are as the animals and all that lives, but as a human being, you are distinct.

Swami Vivekananda

Brahman is like the clay of substance
out of which an infinite variety of articles are fashioned.
As clay, they are all one; but form or manifestation differentiates them. Before every one of them was made,
they all existed potentially in clay, and of course, they are identical substantially; but when formed,
and so long as the form remains, they are separate and different.

Swami Vivekananda

Indian village potters, making kitchen utensils.

The universe is not ruled by arbitrary, temporary martial law.
No force exists that is powerful enough to derail it, or to continue indefinitely on its own path unregulated,
like an outlaw who disrupts all harmony around him. On the contrary, every force must return
to a state of equilibrium along a preordained curve. Waves rise, each to its own level,
with an apparent attitude of relentless rivalry, but only up to a certain point. We can thus understand
the vast serenity of the sea, to which all the waves are connected,
and to which they must all subside in the rhythm of marvelous beauty.

Rabindranath Tagore

Kuri Oasis, in Rajasthan.

The universe is the energy of the soul; and from this energy comes life, consciousness, and the elements.
The universe is the will of the soul; and from this will comes the law of cause and effect.
From the soul one became many; but in the soul many are one.

Mundaka Upanishad

Sangeeth, a girl of six, in Tamil Nadu.

This universe is like an ocean in perfect equilibrium.

A wave cannot rise in one place, without creating a hollow elsewhere.

The sum total of the energy of the universe remains identical from one end to the other.

If you take from one place, you must give elsewhere.

Swami Vivekananda

Varanasi is one of the oldest cities of the world and the most sacred site for Hindus, who come to purify themselves in the Ganges.

Energy is action and movement. All action is movement and all action is energy.

All desire is energy. All feeling is energy. All thought is energy.

All living is energy. All life is energy.

If that energy is allowed to flow without any contradiction,

without any friction, without any conflict, then that energy is boundless, endless.

When there is no friction there are no frontiers to energy.

It is friction which gives energy limitations. So, having once seen this,

why is it that the human being always brings friction into energy?

Why does he create friction in this movement which we call life?

Is pure energy, energy without limitations just an idea to him?

Does it have no reality?

Krishnamurti

A family of itinerant musicians at Jodhpur Fort.

If you see the soul in every living being, you see truly.

If you see immortality in the heart of every mortal being, you see truly.

The Bhagavad Gita

Sharifa, a young woman of the semi-nomadic Mir clan, in Gujarat.
Following pages: Prayer at sunrise, in Varanasi.

14 January

It is through you that the sun shines and the stars shed their lustre, and the earth becomes beautiful.
It is through your blessedness that they all love and are attracted to each other.
You are in all, and you are all.

Swami Vivekananda

What is the soul? The soul is consciousness.

It shines as the light within the heart.

Brihadaranyaka Upanishad

The sacred ghats of Varanasi are thousands of years old.

Our consciousness is not actually yours or mine; it is the consciousness of man,

evolved, grown, accumulated through many, many centuries....

When one realizes this our responsibility becomes extraordinarily important.

Krishnamurti

A Hindu deity guards one of the doors of the temple of Tiruchirappalli, in Tamil Nadu.

There are thousands of lives in one single life.

Svami Prajnanpad

Anna, villager of Maharashtra.

Man progresses, from epoch to epoch, toward the full realization of his soul,
of this soul that is greater than all the riches he can accumulate,
than all the actions he can accomplish and all the theories he can set forth,
this soul that continues onward, never ending in death or dissolution.

Rabindranath Tagore

The palace of Jawainiwas in Jaisalmer.

Nature is forever giving us chance after chance at what we call rebirth and death,
and we, in our folly, in our fear of death, fail to understand that which represents a new journey,
a new page on which to write, and thus to believe in a new beginning for ourselves....
The truth is that my body has come to existence, and that it will cease to exist. I am eternal.

Rev. Parthasarathi Rajagopalachari

A girl of Rajasthan resting in the lap of an elder.

The lamp is empty; the oil is used up.

The tambourine is dead, the dancer lies down,

The fire is out, and no smoke rises from it.

The soul is absorbed into the Unique, and there is no longer a duality.

Kabir

Clay pots allow the villagers to keep water fresh and pure.

In this world there are two orders of being,
the perishable and the imperishable.
The perishable is all that is visible. The imperishable
is the invisible substance of all that is visible.

The Bhagavad Gita

Offering stall next to the temple of Omkareshwar in Madhya Pradesh.

A man is a universe in miniature, and the universe, a giant living body;

the cosmos is similar to a large man,

and a man is similar to a small cosmos; so say the Sufis.

Kabir

Kanchenjunga, in the north of Sikkim, is the third highest summit of the world (8,598 meters).

At our first meeting with beauty, we see it in its gaudy faded finery, jarring us with its garish tones,

its frills and flounces, even its deformed shapes. But when we get to know it better,

the apparent discord reveals itself to us as rhythmic modulations.

At first, we isolate beauty from all that is around it; we detach it from the rest;

but in the end, we understand its harmony with the whole.

Rabindranath Tagore

Every evening, the women of the villages fetch drinking water in copper jars.

The divine music is incessantly going on within ourselves,

but the loud senses drown the delicate music,

which is unlike and infinitely superior to anything we can perceive with our senses.

Mahatma Gandhi

A musician of Rajasthan tunes his instrument for the village party.

What does it matter if we do not understand the exact meaning of the grand harmony?

Is it not like the bow player who touches a string and at once releases every resonance? This is the language

of beauty, this is the caress that comes from the heart of the world and goes straight to our hearts.

Rabindranath Tagore

When a child comes of age, he is entrusted with the care of his younger brothers and sisters so that his parents may travel.

Beauty lies in the total abandonment of the observer and the observed,
and there can be self-abandonment only when there is total austerity.
There is no ladder to climb; there is only the first step
and the first step is the everlasting step.

Krishnamurti

Mana, a young girl of the snake charmer tribe, in Rajasthan.

Does a flower, full of beauty, light and loveliness say, 'I am giving, helping, serving?'
It is! And because it is not trying to do anything it covers the earth.

Krishnamurti

A woman is never seen in public without having arranged her hair just so.
Following pages: The sun sets in Rajasthan.

Man has lost his inner perspective, he measures his greatness by his size
and not by his vital attachment to the infinite; he judges his activity by his own movement
and not by the serenity of perfection, not by the peace that exists in the starry vault,
in the rhythmic dance of incessant creation.

Rabindranath Tagore

There is an orderliness in the universe, there is an unalterable law governing everything and every being that exists or lives.

Mahatma Gandhi

Scene of daily life on the ghats of Varanasi in front of the Ganges.

Order is the very essence of the universe —
the order of birth and death and so on. It is only man that seems to live in disorder, confusion.
He has lived that way since the world began.

Krishnamurti

India possesses the richest biodiversity in the world.

Man must understand that when he cuts himself off from all stimulating and purifying contact with infinity, and no longer relies on it for his subsistence and his health, he risks madness; he tears himself asunder, and divorces himself from his very substance.

Rabindranath Tagore

Women cross the Thar desert on their way to market in Chotane, where they will buy dahi (yogurt).

Do we still not know that the appearance of a seed is in direct contradiction to its true nature? If you submit the seed to a chemical analysis, you would find in it perhaps some carbon, proteins, and many other things, but never the hint of the leaf of a tree.

Rabindranath Tagore

The three tribes of Gujarat can be distinguished by their distinctive jewelry and embroidered clothing.

The freedom of the seed resides in its fulfillment of its dharma, of its nature and its destiny,

which is to become a tree; the failure to achieve this

becomes for the seed a prison.

The sacrifice through which one thing reaches its fulfillment is not a sacrifice that leads to death;

it is the casting off of chains and the attainment of freedom.

Rabindranath Tagore

The nose ring is worn by women of all ages.

Like the silkworm you have built a cocoon around yourself. Who will save you?
Burst your own cocoon and come out as the beautiful butterfly, as the free soul.

Swami Vivekananda

During the religious feast of Ravecchi in the Gujarat, a baby sleeps, wrapped in her mother's shawl.

We must always bear in mind
that we are not going to be free,
but are free already.
Every idea that we are bound is a delusion.
Every idea that we are happy or unhappy
is a tremendous delusion.

Swami Vivekananda

Old and poor pilgrims come to the sacred place of Jaïn of Palitana.

We would be happy to do the millions of things that we are not able to do.
The will is there, but we are not able to fulfill our desire. Thus when we feel a desire,
but we are unable to realize that desire, we undergo a reaction we call suffering.
What is the cause of desire? I am, only me.
As a result, I myself am the cause of all of the suffering that I have known.

Swami Vivekananda

In the heart of the city of Maduraï, the deity of the temple is venerated by more than ten thousand Hindu pilgrims each day.

To understand pleasure is not to deny it.

We are not condemning it or saying it is right or wrong but if we pursue it,

let us do so with our eyes open, knowing that a mind that is all the time seeking pleasure

must inevitably find its shadow in pain.

They cannot be separated, although we run after pleasure and try to avoid pain.

Krishnamurti

A moment of modesty for Priyanka, a young girl of Tamil Nadu.

Man falls from the pursuit of the ideal of plain living and high thinking the moment he wants to multiply his daily wants. Man's happiness really lies in contentment.

Mahatma Gandhi

An animal, a child and an ignoramus are slaves to their desires.

They want to satisfy them immediately, whatever the time, the place or the circumstances...

How can a man be distinguished from them? Before satisfying his desires, a man takes into account the time,

the place and the circumstances, because he is trying to achieve an aim.

Svami Prajnanpad

In every family, the young take care of the old, and vice-versa.

If you wish to free yourself from suffering, you must free yourself from pleasure,
and not free yourself from suffering. Suffering is a reaction.
If you wish to release yourself from suffering,
you must first of all release yourself from pleasure.
Then the suffering will disappear.

Svami Prajnanpad

Shakina, a young girl of the Mir clan in Gujarat.

Satisfy one's desires, certainly, but which ones?

And to what extent?

To determine precisely what I want, and how.

Children? Money? Glory? How?

Svami Prajnanpad

Hot tea is often sipped from a saucer to cool it off.

Our responsibility is no longer to acquire, but to be.

Rabindranath Tagore

The women of Rajasthan are proud of their finery.

As long as the brain, which is so heavily conditioned, is measuring, "the more," "the better," moving psychologically from this to that, it must inevitably bring about a sense of conflict, and this is disord(

Not only the words more and better, but the feeling, the reaction, of achieving, gaining—as long as there is this division, duality, there must be conflict. And out of conflict is disorder.

Krishnamurti

Kalavipayat, a traditional combat sport in Kerala.

We are always comparing what we are with what we should be.

This measuring ourselves all the time against something or someone

is one of the primary causes of conflict. Now why is there any comparison at all?

If you do not compare yourself with another

you will be what you really are.

Krishnamurti

Indian women apply the tika between their eyes as an ornament.

Free yourself from anger and desire, which are the causes of sin and conflict,
and thereby make yourself whole. This is the essence of yoga;
this is the means by which you come to know the soul, and thereby attain the highest spiritual state.
Learn to meditate. Close your eyes; calm your breathing; and focus your attention
on the center of consciousness. Thus you will master the senses, the emotions, and the intellect—
and thereby free yourself from desire and anger.

The Bhagavad Gita

The symbolic meditative pose of a young sadhu, a mendicant ascetic.

Those who are focused on the objects of the senses, become attached to those objects.

From attachment comes desire; and from desire comes anger; from anger comes confusion of mind;

from confusion of mind comes loss of memory; from loss of memory comes loss of intelligence;

and from loss of intelligence comes destruction.

The Bhagavad Gita

———

Tenth-century ruins of the city of Mandu.

When a man is deprived of the foundation that provides him everything,
his poverty loses its best virtue, simplicity, to become no more than disgraceful and sordid.
His wealth is no longer splendid, but becomes merely extravagant.
His appetites no longer remain within natural limits; they no longer have the one goal
of meeting the needs of his life; they become an end in themselves,
setting fire to his existence, and dancing madly by the light of the flames.

Rabindranath Tagore

Perfect for tourist holidays, the houseboat is part of the charm of Kashmir.

As long as you pursue pleasure, you are attached to the sources of pleasure;

and as long as you are attached to the sources of pleasure,

you cannot escape pain and sorrow. The soul shines in the hearts of all living beings.

When you see the soul in others, you forget your own desires and fears,

and lose yourself in the service of others.

The soul shines equally in people on the farthest island, and in people close at hand.

Mundaka Upanishad

In Gujarat, there are more than sixty kinds of cows.

The spiritual can never be attained,
until the material has been extinguished.

Swami Vivekananda

A sadhu on pilgrimage to Nashik.

The absurd denial of the truth is natural in man.

Man does not want to be, but to appear to be.

He does not want to see what he is, but tries only to see himself as the person

other people take him for, when they talk about him.

Svami Prajnanpad

Karna Ram, the man with the longest mustache in the world.

As an individual, a specific entity, you have physical, mental, and nervous limits, among others. If you know your own limits and try to stay within these limits, you are free.

Svami Prajnanpad

Moving freely about the alleyways during the day, the Indian cow produces 1.5 liters of milk each day, and returns to its cowshed at night.

When a man has an idea of what he must be and how he must act,

and undermines this by not ceasing to act in the opposite way,

he must realize that his principles, his beliefs, his ideals,

will inevitably fall prey to hypocrisy and dishonesty.

It is the ideal that begets the opposite of itself.

Krishnamurti

Shanti (Peace), a young dancer of Idukky, in Kerala.

Freedom is a state of mind—not freedom from something.

Krishnamurti

Sadhus lead a solitary life in huts or ashrams, where they receive the teachings of a guru.

This craving for position, for prestige, for power, to be recognized by society as being outstanding in some way, is a wish to dominate others, and this wish to dominate is a form of aggression. And what is the reason for this aggressiveness? It is fear isn't it?

Krishnamurti

Isolated in the Himalayas, the gentle valleys of the Hunza have been protected for centuries.

You must learn how to be lucid in all your actions;

that is, you must not only be aware of the time, the place, and the circumstances,

in which the action takes place, but also of yourself, the player, of your body

and what is happening at any moment.

It is not only a question of seeing things as they are, but of seeing yourself at the same time,

and the reactions that take place within you.

In other words, you absorb the whole thing within you and you become complete.

Svami Prajnanpad

Though formerly itinerant, the potters of Rajasthan have been settled since the partition of India.

How is this dream to be broken,
how shall we wake up from this dream
that we are little men and women,
and all such things?

Swami Vivekananda

The women of Mir, in Gujarat, always wear jewelry
that identifies their semi-nomadic clans.

The only religion that ought to be taught is the religion of fearlessness.

Swami Vivekananda

A woman returns to the village after she has washed her dishes in the pond and her cow has had a drink.

Fear is man's greatest enemy,

and it manifests itself in forms as diverse as shame, jealousy, anger, insolence, arrogance...

What causes fear? Lack of confidence in oneself.

Svami Prajnanpad

In the mountains, woven walls protect cattle from wild animals during the night.

Fear is one of the greatest problems in life. A mind that is caught in fear lives in confusion, in conflict, and therefore must be violent, distorted and aggressive.

Krishnamurti

Priyanka and Sangeetha, sisters from Madras.

First of all, accept yourself.

When you do not accept yourself and imagine yourself to be someone different,

a conflict arises between what you believe you are and what you really are.

Svami Prajnanpad

The elderly remain the guiding spirits of the family.

Everyone is but a manifestation of the Impersonal, the basis of all being, and misery consists in thinking of ourselves as different from this Infinite, Impersonal Being; and liberation consists in knowing our unity with this wonderful Impersonality.

Swami Vivekananda

A young woman washes her cooking pots in the Amballa.

When a man begins to have a vision larger than his own truth,

when he realizes that it is much larger than it at first seemed, he begins to become conscious of his moral nat

His perspective on life necessarily changes, and his will takes the place of his desires.

So comes about the conflict between our inferior self and our superior self,

between our desires and our will, between our greed for objects that appeal to our senses

and the purpose that comes from the bottom of our heart.

Rabindranath Tagore

Tchaï, tea with milk and sugar, is the preferred beverage of India.

*Fear comes from the selfish idea
of cutting one's self off from the universe.*

Swami Vivekananda

Priest pray at sunset on the Ganges in Varanasi.

What we are about to undertake is an expedition together, a journey of discovery into the most secret recesses of our consciousness.
And for such an adventure we must travel light, we cannot burden ourselves with opinions, prejudices, conclusions that is, with all the baggage that we have collected over the past two thousand years or more. Forget everything you know about yourself; forget everything that you have thought about yourself; we are going to set off as if we know nothing.

Krishnamurti

A solitary pilgrim reaches the Bank of the Dead on the Ganges, in Varanasi.

What is the object of jnâna yoga? Freedom.

Freedom from what? Freedom from our imperfections, freedom from the suffering of life.

Why are we unhappy? We are unhappy because we are enslaved. And what are we enslaved by?

The enslavement of nature. Who enslaves us?

We do, ourselves.

Swami Vivekananda

The only way to achieve consciousness
is by concentrating on the physical, the mental, and the spiritual.
Concentration on the powers of the spirit to discover unity
in diversity is called consciousness.
All that draws on unity is moral; all that draws on diversity is immoral.

Swami Vivekananda

Pichaya Manet, international dancer of Pondicherry.

Yoga is concerned with freedom from spiritual disturbance.

The first step in yoga is to engage in introspection,

and thereby understand the inner obstacles that must be overcome.

The purpose of yoga is to weaken the hindrances which obstruct knowledge of the soul.

There are five hindrances: ignorance, egoism, attachment, aversion and tenacity.

Patanjali

Mukesh in a yoga position that he practices every morning.

The question of whether or not there is a God or truth or reality, or whatever you like to call it,

can never be answered by books, by priests, philosophers or saviors.

Nobody and nothing can answer the question

but you yourself and that is why you must know yourself.

Immaturity lies only in total ignorance of self.

To understand yourself is the beginning of wisdom.

Krishnamurti

Saddik, a young groom of the Mir clan in Gujarat.

Knowledge relieves all suffering. Knowledge liberates.

Which knowledge? Chemistry? Physics? Astronomy? Geology?

They help a little, but only a little. The true knowledge is the knowledge of our own nature.

Know yourself. You must know who you are, understand you inner nature.

You must become conscious of this infinite nature in yourself. Then you will break free of your shackles.

Swami Vivekananda

A young Brahmin learns the sacred Hindu texts.
Following pages: Rice paddy in Tamil Nadu, in the rainy season.

The whole universe is bound by the law of causation.

There cannot be anything, any fact—either in the internal or in the external world—

that does not have a cause; and every cause must produce an effect.

Swami Vivekananda

I am imperfect and want to be perfect—this alone is the starting point of my nonviolence. The imperfect will turn perfect when it ceases to be and what is not comes into being.

Acharya Mahaprajna

Pooja, a young girl in Maharashtra.

Man has accepted conflict as an innate part of daily existence
because he has accepted competition, jealousy, greed, acquisitiveness and aggression
as a natural way of life.

Krishnamurti

We are trying to understand violence as a fact, not as an idea,
as a fact which exists in the human being, and the human being is myself.
I must be in a state of mind that demands to see this thing right to the end
and at no point stops and says I will go no further.
Now it must be obvious to me that I am a violent human being...

Krishnamurti

Large cats live wild in the foothills of the Himalayas.

Live your own life.

That is to say, where you are, as you are, with what you are, and with who you are...

Accept the situation in which you find yourself and try, at the same time, to adapt to it.

You cannot escape from it.

Svami Prajnanpad

After a night at sea, the fishermen of Kerala get yesterday's news.

The idea of a duty to understand violence engenders for me

a great vitality and passion for knowledge.

But to transcend this violence, I need not repress it, nor deny it, nor say to myself:

It has become a part of me, I can do nothing about it; or, I wish to reject it.

I must observe it, study it, enter into it intimately,

and for that purpose I need neither condemn it nor justify it.

And yet, it is this that we do.

I would ask you, then, to suspend for an instant your judgments on the subject.

Krishnamurti

In the town of Mandu, two women return from a trip to the watering hole.

All the responsibility of good and evil is on you. This is the great hope. What I have done, that I can undo.

Swami Vivekananda

A painter of miniatures in Jodhpur.

I am myself.
The other is simply something else.
I am what I am.
If I am a demon, very well then I am a demon.
That is all.

Svami Prajnanpad

Two timid young girls near the Pakistani border.

Not only must we be aware of the nature and structure of the problem
and see it completely,
but meet it as it arises and resolve it immediately,
so that it does not take root in the mind.
If one allows a problem to endure for a month or a day,
or even for a few minutes, it distorts the mind.

Krishnamurti

The growth of cities and the rise in the standard of living makes the development of infrastructure difficult.

There is no weapon more powerful in achieving the truth than acceptance of oneself.

Svami Prajnanpad

Before marriage, young girls of Gujarat reveal their faces without hesitation.

It is only when we give complete attention to a problem,

and solve it immediately——never carrying it over to the next day,

the next minute——that there is solitude.

To have inward solitude and space is very important

because it implies freedom to be, to go, to function, to fly.

Krishnamurti

One of the strengths of India is its devoted laborers, as in this textile workshop in Maduraï.

Such awareness is like living with a snake in the room;

you watch its every movement, you are very, very sensitive to the slightest sound it makes.

Such a state of attention is total energy;

in such awareness the totality of yourself is revealed in an instant.

Krishnamurti

Krishna, Bharata Natyan dancer in Ahmadabad.

Contemplation is seeing the here and now.

Svami Prajnanpad

A grandfather in Aravalli cultivates his field while entertaining his grandchildren.

To live completely, fully, in the moment is to live with what is, the actual, without any sense of condemnation or justification——then you understand it so totally that you are finished with it.

When you see clearly the problem is solved.

Krishnamurti

A woman's finery changes according to her region and clan.
Following pages: In the Kuri oasis, after three years of drought, the villagers finally discover water in the pond.

If you are in the moment, you are in the infinite.

Svami Prajnanpad

Life is an aspiration. Its mission is to strive after perfection, which is self-fulfillment. The ideal must not be lowered because of our weaknesses or imperfections.

Mahatma Gandhi

Shanti, dancer of Kerala, in a gesture of Bharata Natyan.

What is change?

One form appears, and another disappears.

Can we say that the butterfly used to be a caterpillar?

A substance in the caterpillar takes on the form of the butterfly.

Svami Prajnanpad

In the villages, a baby sling is quite useful in keeping tabs on a sleeping baby when taking care of daily tasks.

You are never alone because you are full of all the memories, all the conditioning,

all the mutterings of yesterday; your mind is never clear of all the rubbish it has accumulated.

To be alone, you must die to the past.

When you are alone, totally alone, not belonging to any family, any nation, any culture,

any particular continent, there is that sense of being an outsider.

The man who is completely alone in this way is innocent and it is this innocence that frees the mind from sor

Krishnamurti

The renunciation of the material world is a Hindu ideal.

Life is like a garden. Quite naturally, leaves wither and flowers fade.

Only if we clear the decay of the past

then and there can we really enjoy the beauty of the new leaves and flowers.

Likewise, we must clear the murkiness of past bad experiences from our minds.

Life is remembrance in forgetfulness.

Forgive what ought to be forgiven; forget what ought to be forgotten.

Let us embrace life with renewed vigor...

We should be able to face every moment of life with renewed expectation, like a freshly blossomed flower.

Mata Amritanandamayi

The Hunza Valley in north Pakistan during the month of May.

A mind that is burdened with the past is a sorrowful mind.

Krishnamurti

A scrap dealer clears a way through the congested streets of Maduraï.

We would rather cling to the known than face the unknown—
the known being our house, our furniture, our family,
our character, our work, our knowledge, our fame, our loneliness, our gods—
that little thing that moves around incessantly within itself,
with its own limited embittered existence.

Krishnamurti

A security guard at break time.

Death is extraordinarily like life,
when we know how to live.
You cannot live without dying.
You cannot live if you do not die
psychologically every minute.

Krishnamurti

In Kerala, kalavipayat, formerly a form of physical training for war,
has now become a theatrical art.

All of our selfish impulses, all of our personal desires, obscure our true vision of the soul,
as they only point out our shabby ego. When we are aware of our soul,
we perceive the inner life that surpasses our ego
and that has profound affinities with the Whole.

Rabindranath Tagore

Smoking shillum and opium is only for those uninterested in an active life.

Do men fear sleep?

One prepares the bed for sound sleep.

Sleep is temporary death. Death is longer sleep.

If the man dies while yet alive, he need not grieve over others' death.

One's experience is evident with or without the body, as in waking, dream, and sleep.

Then why should one desire continuance of the bodily shackles?

Let man find out his undying Self and die and be immortal and happy.

Sri Ramana Maharshi

In this turbulent country, every aspect of life can be encountered on the street.

The Hindu believes that he is a spirit.

He believes that the sword cannot pierce him, that fire cannot burn him,

that water cannot dissolve him, that air cannot dry him out.

He believes that the soul is a circle whose circumference has no limits, but whose center is situated in the body.

Death signifies the transference of this center of a body to another.

We are the children of God.

Matter is our servant.

Swami Vivekananda

A group of pilgrims from Tamil Nadu in prayer by the Ganges in Varanasi.

To know our soul apart from our ego

is the first step toward accomplishing the supreme deliverance.

It is necessary that we know with absolute certainty that in essence we are spirit.

And we can only arrive at this knowledge if we render ourselves masters of our ego,

if we rise above all pride, all appetite, all fear, by knowing that material losses and the

death of the body can never take away the truth and the greatness of our soul.

Rabindranath Tagore

Flowers and incense, offerings to the gods.

Man is setting out to satisfy needs that mean more to him
than simply nourishment and clothing.
He is embarking on a rediscovery of himself.
The history of man is that of his voyage toward the unknown,
in the search for the realization of his immortal Self, of his soul.

Rabindranath Tagore

Jain ascetics on pilgrimage.

The Upanishad tells us: Know the soul that is your own.

In other words: Realize the grand unique principle of the whole that is in all men.

Rabindranath Tagore

Jain temples are open to all faiths and communities.

The very essence of the Hindu Philosophy
is that man is a spirit, and has a body,
and not that man is a body and
may have a spirit also.

Swami Vivekananda

Benediction of peace.

There is no master, there is no instructor,
there is no person to tell you what you must do.

Krishnamurti

Offerings of the faithful to a Jain deity, in a posture of meditation.

We must refuse to be lifted off our feet.

A drowning man cannot save others.

Mahatma Gandhi

In the Gulf of Bengal, young newlyweds take in the sea.

To expect something is to look for something pleasant.
Searching for the pleasurable is a form of denial.
You cannot expect anything, because the expectation is within you,
and what you are waiting for is dependent on external forces.

Svami Prajnanpad

In Tamil Nadu, 80 percent of children go to school.

Adaptability is not imitation.

It means power of resistance and assimilation.

Mahatma Gandhi

At the feast of Pushkar, a camel fair gives the village communities a chance to meet.

Do not believe a thing simply because it has been said.

Do not put your faith in traditions only because they have been honored by many generations.

Do not believe a thing because the general opinion believes it to be true or because it has been said repeatedl(

Do not believe a thing because of the single witness of one of the sages of antiquity.

Do not believe a thing because the probabilities are in its favor,

or because you are in the habit of believing it to be true.

Do not believe in that which comes to your imagination,

thinking that it must be the revelation of a superior Being.

Believe nothing that binds you to the sole authority of your masters or priests.

That which you have tried yourself, which you have experienced, which you have recognized as true,

and which will be beneficial to you and to others;

believe that, and shape your conduct to it.

Buddha

The religious ceremonies during the full moon of November are the most important for Hindus.

We gain our freedom when we realize our most true nature.

The man who is an artist gains his artistic freedom when he discovers the true ideal of art.

Rabindranath Tagore

Sculpture of celestial beauty, in the temple of Tiruchirappalli.

It is not a question of belief.
Stop believing in that which is;
this is what is taught in jnâna yoga.
Believe in no other,
stop believing in that which is;
this is the first stage. Dare to be rational.
Dare to follow reason where it may take you.

Swami Vivekananda

A Gujarat peasant lying on his woven cot after milking his cows.

Does distress and despair, melancholy, and madness come from God?

Does pleasure and prosperity, joy, and reason come from God?

Was the human form, in all its beauty, designed by God?

Does God give each person a distinct character and appearance?

Does God give men and women the ability to think?

Does God give human beings the urge to worship?

Does God plant the notions of truth and untruth in the human mind?

Does God decide when human beings should die?

Does God offer the hope of immortality?

Atharva Veda

During the full moon of November, the villagers of Rajasthan purify themselves in the sacred water of the lake of Pushkar.

Truth has no path, and that is the beauty of truth, it is living.

Krishnamurti

Evening: the daily gathering of water allows the women of the village to meet at the well.

We should never try to follow another's path for that is his way, not yours.
When that path is found, you have nothing to do but fold your arms
and the tide will carry you to freedom.
Therefore when you find it, never swerve from it.
Your way is the best for you,
but that is no sign it is the best for another.

Swami Vivekananda

The priest of the temple of Mandu in his banyan arbor.

When you believe that the truth is living, moving, that it does not have one home or rest in any temple, mosque, or church, in any religion, master or philosopher—in short, that nothing can lead you to it— you will see also that you are this living thing in every respect; it is your anger, your brutality, your violence, your despair. It is the agony and the pain that you live through. The truth is in the comprehension of all of this; you cannot comprehend it unless you are determined to see it in your life.

Krishnamurti

The veil allows the village women of India to preserve their privacy as they fetch water at the well.

As long as there is division in any form
there must be conflict.
You are responsible, not only to your children,
but to the rest of humanity.
Unless you deeply understand this, not through words or ideas or the intellect,
but feel this in your blood, in your way of looking at life, in your actions,
you are supporting organized murder which is called war.

Krishnamurti

In all religions of the world you will find it claimed that there is unity within us.
Being one with divinity, there cannot be any further progress in that sense.
Knowledge means finding this unity.

Swami Vivekananda

Among the young, clothing is more a question of personal preference than tradition.

When you look at that unchanging Existence
from the outside, you call it God;
and when you look at it from the inside,
you call it yourself. It is but one.

Swami Vivekananda

Evening prayer at the mosque Aurangzeb, in Varanasi.

Where does the soul go after death? Where could the earth fall to?
Where can the soul go? Where is it not already?
The great cornerstone of Vedantism is the recognition of Self.
Man, have faith in yourself. The soul is the same in every one.
It is all purity and perfection and the more pure and perfect we [you] are
the more purity and perfection you will see.

Swami Vivekananda

A return to the village after a day watching over sheep, in the mountains of Aravalli.

Even at the gate of death, in the greatest danger,

in the thick of the battlefield,

at the bottom of the ocean, on the tops of the highest mountains,

in the thickest of the forest, tell yourself,

"I am He, I am He."

Swami Vivekananda

The universal power that manifests itself in the universal law

is at one with our true power.

Rabindranath Tagore

In the mountains of Aravalli, the villagers grind corn to make flat cakes.

This glorious soul we must believe in. Out of that will come power.

Whatever you think, that you will be. If you think yourselves weak, weak you will be;

if you think yourselves strong, strong you will be; if you think yourselves impure, impure you will be;

if you think yourselves pure, pure you will be. This teaches us not to think ourselves as weak, but as strong,

omnipotent, omniscient. No matter that I have not expressed it yet, it is in me.

All knowledge is in me, all power, all purity, and all freedom. Why cannot I express this knowledge?

Because I do not believe in it. Let me believe in it, and it must and will come out.

This is what the idea of the Impersonal teaches.

Swami Vivekananda

Monsoon rains on the jetty of the Mosque of haji Ali, in Mumbai.

Never say, O Lord, I am a miserable sinner. Who will help you?
It is you who must help the universe.

Swami Vivekananda

Yoga is a daily discipline that brings the mental and the physical into harmony.

When a man possesses in his being the notion of God, that is the miracle of miracles.

Rabindranath Tagore

For Hindus, the rising and setting of the sun are moments given to prayer.

In the song of the rushing torrent,

hold onto the joyful assurance:

I will become the sea.

And this is not a vain supposition;

it is absolute humility, because it is the truth.

Rabindranath Tagore

After school, children meet at the pond of Dasada, in Gujarat, at dusk.

The phrase 'to meditate' does not only mean to examine, observe, reflect, question, weigh; it also has, in the Sanskrit, a more profound meaning, which is "to become."

Krishnamurti

India has a population close to 1.1 million inhabitants, 30 percent of whom live in cities.

Every day a man must solve the problem

of widening the field of his life and adjusting his burdens.

These are too complex and numerous for him to carry himself,

but he knows that by being methodical he can lighten the load.

When the burdens are too complicated and difficult to manage, he must understand the reason:

he has not found a system that will put everything in place and distribute the weight he carries more evenly

The search for this system is actually the search for the whole, for synthesis;

it is our effort to create harmony, thanks to an interior adaptation,

in the heterogeneous complex of exterior material.

Rabindranath Tagore

Along a narrow route through the Thar desert, a group taxi, providing for the livestock of the villages during a period of drought, attempts to overtake a truck filled with forage.

To grow is to go beyond what you are today.

Stand up as yourself. Do not imitate.

Do not pretend to have achieved your goal, and do not try to cut corners.

Just try to grow.

Svami Prajnanpad

Women have an important place in the political life of the country and within the family.

Never under any circumstances ask "how."
When you use the word "how" you really want someone to tell you what to do,
some guide, some system, someone to lead you by the hand so that you lose your freedom,
your capacity to observe, your own activities, your own thoughts, your own way of life.

Krishnamurti

Gita, a young girl of the Kharapat Rabari community in Gujarat.

I do not want my house to be walled in on all sides and my windows to be stuffed.

I want the cultures of all the lands to blow about my house as freely as possible.

But I refuse to be blown off my feet by any.

Mahatma Gandhi

After the hot season, in late afternoon, the square of the village of Amballa livens up.

Find the Unique and possess the Whole.

This truly is our highest, most sublime privilege.

It is in the law of this unity that is, as long as we understand it,

our immutable force. Its living principle is the force that resides in truth—

Truth is one.

Svami Prajnanpad

Sita, a young girl of Rajasthan, at the village well.

To go from opinion to perception,

from imagination to fact, from illusion to reality,

from something that is not there,

to something that is;

that is the way forward.

Svami Prajnanpad

Truth resides in the heart of every man.

And it is there that he must seek it, in order to be guided by it so that,

at the least, it will appear to him.

But we do not have the right to force others to see the Truth in our way.

Mahatma Gandhi

In the villages, the end of each day is marked by milking.

Your way is very good for you, but not for me.
My way is good for me, but not for you.

Swami Vivekananda

The sadhus follow the teachings of either Vishnu or Shiva, which are in turn divided into many branches.

A diamond is lost in the mud;
all are seeking it.
Some go to the East—or to the West,
Wishing to find it.
Is it lost in the river?
Or in the rocks?
Kabîr, your servant, appreciates it
for its just value.
He will take it away,
warmly sheltered
in a corner of his heart.

Kabir

A village woman sells offerings at the entrance to the temple of Ranakpur.

The person who can wear the mantle of a Master

is one who is devoted to the cause of non-violence and non-possession

who is driven by the quest for truth and the right perspective,

who is capable of solving his own emotional and mental problems and

who can show others the way to overcome their emotional and mental problems.

Acharya Mahaprajna

The guru Manashuwargiri gives instruction to a few disciples in Jodhpur.

Nature's law dictates that, in order to survive, bees must work together.

As a result, they instinctively possess a sense of social responsibility.

They have no constitution, no law, no police, no religion or moral training but,

because of their nature, the whole colony survives.

We human beings have a constitution, laws and a police force.

We have religion, remarkable intelligence, and hearts with a great capacity to love.

We have many extraordinary qualities but, in actual practice,

I think we are behind those small insects.

In some ways, I feel that we are poorer than the bees.

His Holiness the XIVth Dalaï Lama

A winter morning in Varanasi.

The supreme being impregnates all, and, by consequence, is the goodness innate in every thing.

To be truly united with all in knowledge, love, and service, and thus to realize the Self in the omnipresent Go

is the essence of good. This is the keystone of the Upanishad teaching: Life is immense.

Rabindranath Tagore

Pooja, in the monsoon winds at the exit of a temple.

The human soul travels from the law to love,
from discipline to freedom,
from the moral plane to the spiritual plane.

Rabindranath Tagore

Procession around the temple of Ravecchi in Gujarat.

Perceive the souls through the soul and you will become the Supreme soul...

There are two sides of the consciousness: the soul and the Supreme Soul...

one the seed and the other, entirety. You must have seen how small the seed of the banyan tree is.

You must also have seen how expansive the tree is.

It is difficult to even imagine that such a small seed can become so big.

The soul is the seed of a banyan tree and the Supreme Soul its development...

Acharya Mahaprajna

When the mind and intellect developed, man asked,

Who am I? Who is it before me?

The search for reality began...

Moving one step towards finding the answer to the question,

Who am I, we brought consciousness from outside to inside.

Wisdom turned the direction of the consciousness within and

we perceived our soul.

The journey of the soul in the outer world was over and the journey within had begun.

Acharya Mahaprajna

The sheep-herding clans of Gujarat flock to the temple of Ravecchi.

So long as you think you have the least difference from God, fear will seize you,
but when you have known that you are He, that there is no difference, entirely no difference, that you are H
all of Him, and the whole of Him, all fear ceases. Therefore, dare to be free,
dare to go as far as your thought leads, and dare to carry that out in your life.

Swami Vivekananda

Choreography of Pichaya Manet at Jantar Mantar, the astronomical observatory of the eighteenth century that worked out astrology, essential to every life.

Ever tell yourself, I am He.

These are words that will burn up the dross that is in the mind, words that will bring out the tremendous ene

which is within you already, the infinite power which is sleeping in your heart.

Swami Vivekananda

Kohl protects children from evil spirits.

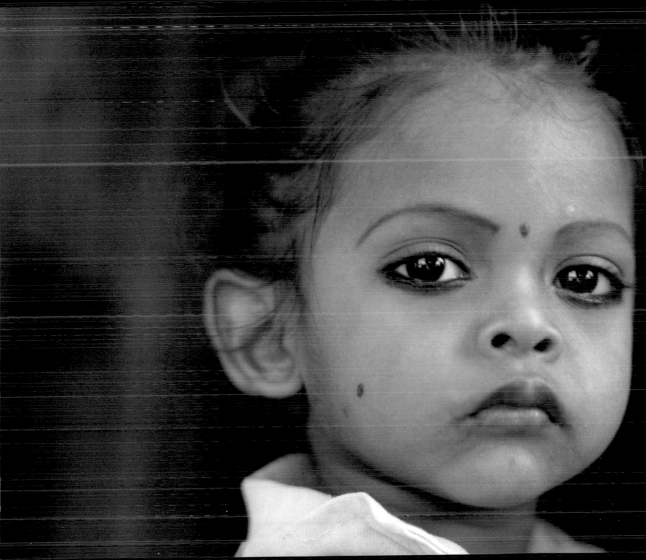

Wise people are concerned only with what lies behind all these things.

Just as bees fly from one blossom to another, looking only for the essence of each one,

wise people look only for the essence of every person they meet.

Wise people, who know and understand the soul, are indifferent to both pleasure and pain;

they have risen above sensations. They are indifferent to the past and the future; they have risen above time.

They are indifferent to danger; they have risen above fear.

Wise people know that what is here, is also there;

that what was, will also be.

They see unity, not division.

Katha Upanishad

Scene of rural life in Kerala.

With closed eyes, I have come to this last thought:

even while I am unconscious in sleep, the dance of life will continue

in the silent field of my sleeping body, in the same rhythm as the stars above.

My heart beats, my blood courses through my arteries,

and the millions of atoms that live in my body will vibrate in time with the harp

that quivers under the fingers of the great Master.

Rabindranath Tagore

A child of the shepherding Rabari tribe in Gujarat.
Following pages: At the temple of Tirumala in the Andhra Pradesh.

20 May

The outward freedom that we shall attain will only be in exact proportion to the inward freedom to which we may have grown at any given moment.

Mahatma Gandhi

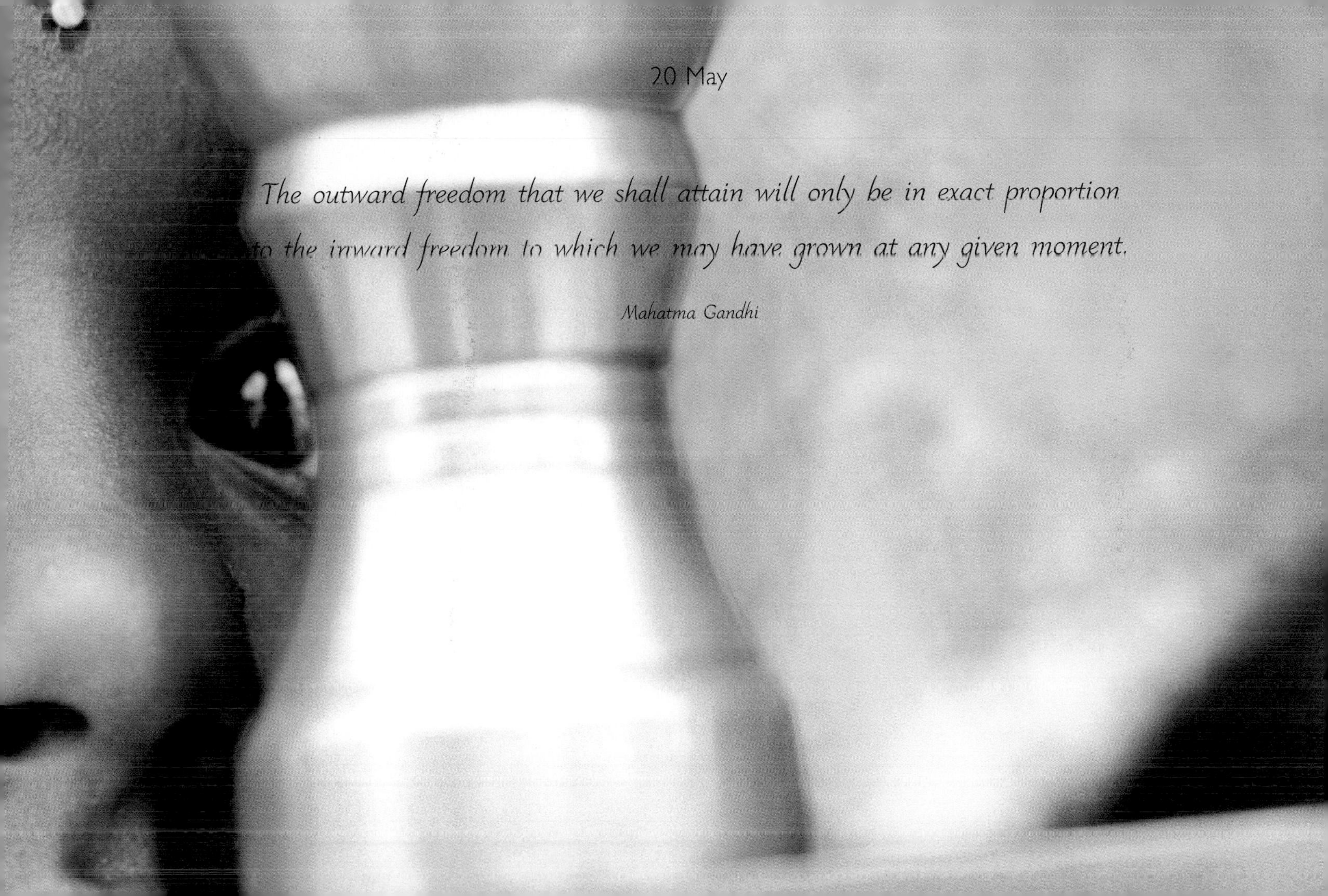

With the clouds hanging in the air above the trees,
and the birds falling silent before the storm,
this morning brings forth serious reflection,
bringing into question the entirety of existence,
the gods themselves, and all human activity.

Krishnamurti

To die in Varanasi is the most cherished wish in every Hindu heart.

Very few people in this world can reason normally.

There is a terrible tendency to accept all that is said, all that is read, and to accept it without question.

Only he who is ready to question, to think for himself, will find the truth!

To understand the currents of a river,

he who wishes to know the truth must enter the water.

Nisargadatta

Reflection of the Golden Temple, in Amritsar, the Sikhs' most venerated sanctuary.

You have to stand against the whole world although you may have to stand alone.

You have to stare the world in the face although the world may look at you with a bloodshot eye.

Do not fear.

Trust that little thing in you which resides in the heart and says:

forsake friends, wife, all, but testify to that for which you have lived and for which you have to die.

Mahatma Gandhi

Ramesh, a young student.

Strength does not come from physical capacity. It comes from an indomitable will.

Mahatma Gandhi

On the east coast, the site of Mahabalipuram.

Fearlessness is the first requirement of spirituality.

Cowards can never be moral.

Mahatma Gandhi

A sadhu, in the Himachal Pradesh.

My work will be finished if I succeed in carrying conviction to the human family,

that every man or woman, however weak in body,

is the guardian of his or her self-respect and liberty, and that this defence prevails,

though the world be against the individual resister.

Mahatma Gandhi

Gita, a young village woman of Gujarat.

True morality consists not in following
the well-beaten track,
but in finding out the true path for ourselves
and in fearlessly following it.

Mahatma Gandhi

Sacred baths at Sonepur.

The purity of life is the highest and most authentic art to follow.

Mahatma Gandhi

Chapati, a bread made of wheat or millet, accompanies every meal in the north.

In Sanskrit, one calls the bird twice born.

And this name is also given to the man who submits for at least twelve years

to the discipline of mastering his self and the noble thought, who emerges from it with simple needs,

with a pure heart, and ready to take upon himself all the responsibilities of life

in a broad and disinterested spirit. One estimates that this man is born again from the blind envelopment

of the ego to the freedom of the life of the soul,

that he has entered into lively connection with his environment,

that he has become one with the Whole.

Rabindranath Tagore

Meditation at Varanasi.

The human voice can never reach the distance
that is covered by the still small voice of conscience.

Mahatma Gandhi

In the villages, under the trees is the place to meet at the end of the day.

Chitragupta, who is supposed to be writing out our deeds in an account book
is no other than the conscious and unconscious parts of our mind.
The Lord of Law, to whom we have to render the account,
is the Soul within us.

Gopal Singh

A porter waits in his cart for his clients.

The main purpose of life is to live rightly, think rightly, act rightly.
The soul must languish when we give all our thought to the body.

Mahatma Gandhi

Village **women** spend two to three hours each day drawing water and **collecting** wood to cook.

Man lives in confusion and fear until he discovers the uniformity of the law in nature;

until then the world is a stranger to him.

And yet, the law discovered is only the perception of the harmony between reason,

which is the soul of man, and the play of nature.

It is the bond that unites man to the world he lives in.

When he discovers it, man feels an intense joy, because he realizes himself in his environment.

To understand this is to find something to which we belong,

and it is the discovery of ourselves outside ourselves that gives us joy.

Rabindranath Tagore

On the coast of Kerala, fishermen put in at Chennai after a night at sea.

By the term religion, I am using it
in its broadest sense, meaning thereby self realization
or knowledge of the self.

Mahatma Gandhi

Sumar Ram, sixty-five years old, in Kuldhara.

By education I mean an all-round drawing out of the best in a child and man—body, mind, and spirit.

Mahatma Gandhi

Shakina, a young girl of the Mir clan in Gujarat.

If this individuality is wiped away, the creative joy that crystallized it disappears,

even if no material was lost, even if no atom was destroyed.

And if it is lost, it is also a loss for the entire world. It is particularly precious because it is not universal.

Rabindranath Tagore

A young bride, whose husband was chosen by her parents, the day after their wedding.

Most parents unfortunately think they are responsible for their children

and their sense of responsibility takes the form of telling them what they should do,

what they should not do, what they should become and what they should not become.

The parents want their children to have a secure position in society. What they call responsibility is part of that

pectability they worship; and it seems to me that where there is respectability there is no order.

Do you call that care and love?

Krishnamurti

Kashmir, a vast region of the Himalayas that lies between Pakistan and India, is inhabited by numerous ethnic groups such as the nomadic shepherds of Gujjar.

Allow your son to say foolish things.

They are foolish things from your point of view, but when he speaks agree with him.

Say, all right, yes, I understand what you mean. Yes, I agree. Once he has expressed his opinion,

then try to show him that there are inconsistencies in some of what he is saying.

Svami Prajnanpad

In Kashmir, a Gujjar child of a nomadic shepherd tribe is weary after a long day's walk.

A child must be brought up to understand the word no. He should be taught yes first of all, then, yes and no, then no and yes, in such a way that he gradually comes to realize, that there is really only n

A child's education is learning to understand no, and this enables him to grow.

Growing up means accepting the concept of no.

Svami Prajnanpad

A child giving an offering at the temple of Tirumala.

I hold that true education of the intellect can only come through a proper exercise
and training of the bodily organs, e.g., hands, feet, eyes, ears, nose, etc.
In other words an intelligent use of the bodily organs in a child provides
the best and quickest way of developing his intellect.
But unless the development of the mind and body goes hand in hand
with a corresponding awakening of the soul,
the former alone would prove to be a poor lopsided affair.
By spiritual training I mean education of the heart.

Mahatma Gandhi

The bamboo flute is a common instrument for both classical and folk music. Following pages: Meeting at the well, dusk.

What is the world? It is the earth below and the sky above and the air in space that connects them.

What is light? It is fire below and the sun above – and the lightning that connects them.

What is education? It is the teacher above and the disciple below – and the wisdom that connects them.

Taittiriya Upanishad

The first condition of humaneness is a little humility and a little diffidence about the correctness of one's conduct and a little receptiveness.

Mahatma Gandhi

At Tiruchirappalli, an elephant makes for a light moment among pilgrims in the surrounding walls of the temple.

You can live with few clothes or with one meal a day, but that is not simplicity.
So be simple, don't live in a complicated way, contradictory and so on, just be simple inwardly.

Krishnamurti

Dried cow dung is used throughout the country as fuel for the cooking fire.

If a man does not of his own free will put himself last among his creatures, there is no salvation for him.

Mahatma Gandhi

The kitchen, one of the main rooms of the house, where drinking water is stored in clay pots.

Hold the reins of your mind, as you would hold the reins of a restive horse.

Svetasvatara Upanishad

The walls of the palace of Rajasthan are decorated with frescoes.

When you abandon every desire that rises up within you,

and when you become content with things as they are, then you experience inner peace.

When your mind is untroubled by misfortune, when you desire no pleasures,

when your emotions are tranquil, and when you are free from fear and anger,

then you experience inner calm. When you are free from all attachments,

when you are indifferent to success and failure,

then you experience inner serenity.

When you can withdraw your senses from pleasures of the senses,

just as a tortoise withdraws its limbs,

then you experience inner wisdom.

The Bhagavad Gita

On the ghats of Vanarasi, where the buffaloes gather, sacred life and daily life coexist.

We have at the present moment everybody claiming the right of conscience
without going through any discipline whatsoever
that there is so much untruth being delivered to a bewildered world.
Truth is not to be found by anybody who has not got a sense of humility.
If you would swim on the bosom of this ocean of Truth
you reduce yourself to a zero.

Mahatma Gandhi

The Buddhist area of Sanchi (second century B.C.) has been preserved from destruction thanks to its isolation high up on a hill.

What is then worth having?

Mukti, freedom.

Swami Vivekananda

Earth, Water, Fire, Air, and Ether are the five base elements.

Being human,

I feel profoundly the necessity of putting an end to violence,

and I will make sure to put an end to it in myself.

Krishnamurti

Going home from school in Tamil Nadu.

Violence is not merely killing another.

It is violence when we use a sharp word,

when we make a gesture to brush away a person,

when we obey because there is fear.

So violence isn't merely organized butchery in the name of God,

in the name of society, or country.

Violence is much more subtle, much deeper,

and we are inquiring into the very depths of violence.

Krishnamurti

Animals are a part of life in both city and countryside.

Guard your tongue, for it is highly dangerous;
unguarded words can cause terrible distress.
A single bad word can destroy a vast quantity of good.
A wound caused by fire will eventually heal;
but a wound caused by the tongue leaves a scar that never heals.

Valluvar

Lakshmi, a young woman of Gujarat.

I declare out loud to whoever wants to believe me:

I have no word in my mouth

that is not in your heart!

Kabir

Appi, twelve years old.

All things are linked together through cause and effect. There is no such thing as an accident. When we cannot find the link between cause and effect in an event, we call it an accident.

Svami Prajnanpad

On the ghats of Varanasi, the village painter embellishes a water tower.

There will have to be rigid and iron discipline
before we achieve anything great and enduring,
and that discipline will not come by mere academic argument
and appeal to reason and logic.
Discipline is learnt in the school of adversity.

Mahatma Gandhi

Krihsna, dancer of Bharat Natyam, in Ahmadabad.

To conquer the subtle passions
seems to me to be far harder than the
physical conquest of the world by the force of arms.

Mahatma Gandhi

A yoga posture.

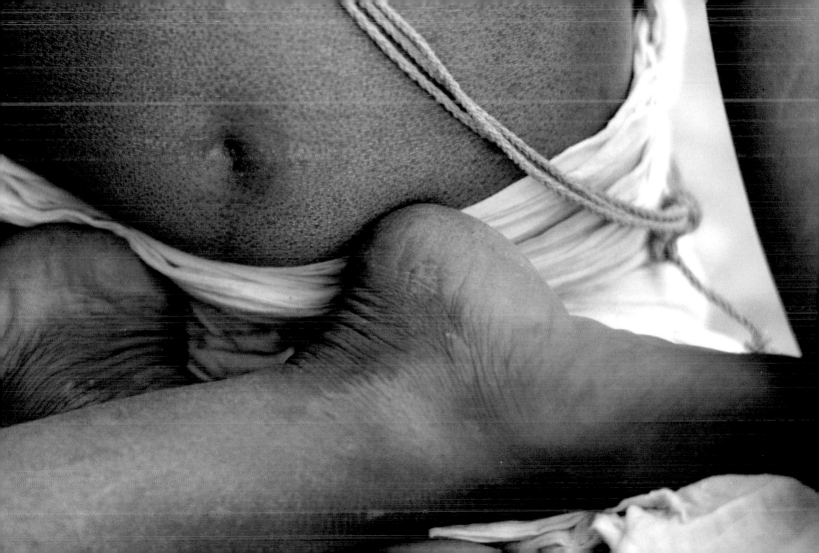

Watching and listening are a great art.
By watching and listening we learn infinitely more than we do from any books.
Books are necessary, but watching and listening sharpen your senses.

Krishnamurti

Pooja has been taken out of the weaving workshop by the RIDE Association to attend school.

*The healing of the mind takes place gradually on contact with nature,
with the orange on the branch, the blade of grass eating its way into the cement,
and the hills hidden by the clouds.*

Krishnamurti

Banyan roots.

Meditation is one of the greatest arts in life, perhaps the greatest,
and one cannot possibly learn it from anybody else,
that is the beauty of it.
It has no technique and therefore no authority.
When you learn about yourself, watch yourself, watch the way you walk,
how you eat, what you say, the gossip, the hate, the jealousy—
if you are aware of all that in yourself, without any choice,
that is part of meditation.

Krishnamurti

During the livestock fair of Sonepur, a peasant relaxes on an improvised litter.

Man cannot be broken down into emotions, intellect, or action.

Man is a whole.

When these three elements of intellect, feelings, and action are in harmony, they make up man.

Svami Prajnanpad

Mukesh, at the entrance to the temple of Omkareshwar.

Meditation is movement without any motive, without words, and the activity of thought.
It must be something that is not deliberately set about.
Only then is it a movement within the infinite, measureless to man, without a goal, without an end,
without a beginning. And that has a strange action in daily life, because all life is one,
and then becomes sacred.

Krishnamurti

Under the shade of a tree, at the feast of Ravecchi.

Religion is a realization, not talk, not doctrines,
nor theories, however beautiful all these may be.
Religion is being and becoming, not hearing or acknowledging.
It is not an intellectual assent;
but the transformation of one's whole life.

Swami Vivekananda

After their prayer on the Ganges, pilgrims take a little water of the sacred river. Following pages: The Thar desert, in Rajasthan, the largest state in India and the most sparsely populate

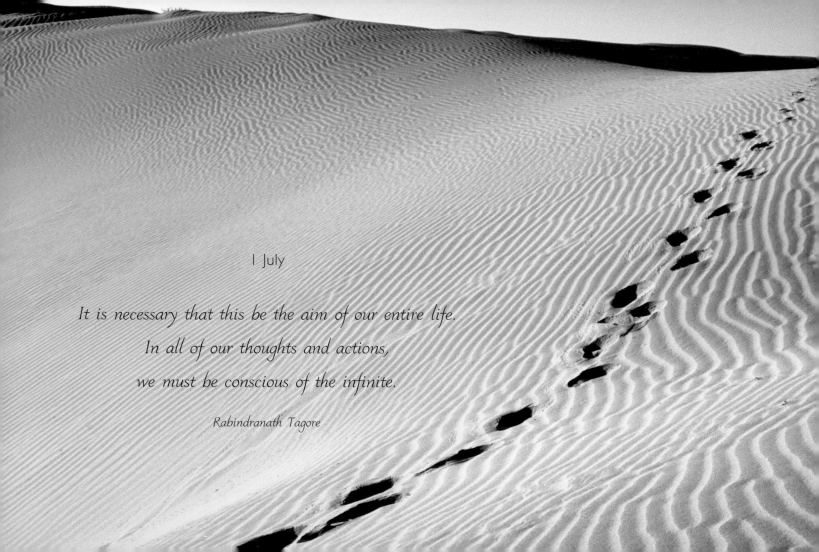

1 July

It is necessary that this be the aim of our entire life.
In all of our thoughts and actions,
we must be conscious of the infinite.

Rabindranath Tagore

There is a little stump of a tree. What does the child see?

A ghost, with hands stretched out, ready to grab him.

Suppose a man comes from the corner of the street, wanting to meet his sweetheart;

he sees that stump of the tree as the girl. A policeman coming from the street corner sees the stump as a thie

The thief sees it as a policeman. It is the same stump of a tree that was seen in various ways.

The stump is the reality, and the visions of the stump are the projections of the various minds.

There is one Being, this Self; It neither comes nor goes.

Swami Vivekananda

An acacia, the only tree that can live in the desert.

Do you know that even when you look at a tree and say,

'That is an oak,' or 'that is a banyan tree,'

the naming of the tree, which is botanical knowledge, has so conditioned your mind

that the word comes between you and actually seeing the tree?

To enter in contact with the tree you have to put your hand on it

and the word will not help you touch it.

Krishnamurti

Called Ammachial, the mother of trees, this tree dates from the arrival of the Portuguese (1498), and is the oldest in Cochin. It is honored by its inhabitants during the festival of trees in su

Life is very real—

life is not an abstraction—our problems begin when we encounter it only through images.

Krishnamurti

Varanasi, where commerce flourishes and the traffic is intense, attracts more pilgrims than any other city in India.

The like and dislike is the result of my culture, my training, my associations,
my inclinations, my acquired and inherited characteristics.
It is from that center that I observe and make my judgments,
and the observer is separate from the thing he observes.

Krishnamurti

In Mumbai, a vender offers a garland of jasmine flowers in the monsoon rains.

No one can understand the sound of a drum,

without understanding both the drum and the drummer.

No one can understand the sound of a conch shell,

without understanding the shell and the one who blows it.

No one can understand the sound of a lute,

without understanding both the lute and the one who plays it.

As there can be no water without the sea, no touch without the skin,

no smell without the nose, no taste without the tongue, no sound without the ear,

no thought without the mind, no work without hands, and no walking without feet,

so there can be nothing without the soul.

Brihadaranyaka Upanishad

Musician of the Achalnath Mahadev temple, in Jodhpur.

The state of mind is a vicious circle. It creates problems for itself, and then tries to resolve them.

Svami Prajnanpad

Thought is crooked
because it can invent anything
and see things that are not there.
It can perform the most extraordinary tricks,
therefore it cannot be depended upon.

Krishnamurti

The cow is the mainstay of agriculture.

Have you ever tried living with yourself?

If so, you will begin to see that yourself is not a static state,

it is a fresh living thing.

And to live with a living thing your mind must also be alive.

And it cannot be alive if it is caught in opinions, judgements, and values.

Krishnamurti

Daily gymnastics of the dairy community in Varanasi.

How can we be free to look and learn when our minds from the moment we are born
to the moment we die are shaped by a particular culture
in the narrow pattern of "me?"
For centuries we have been conditioned by nationality, caste, class, tradition,
religion, language, education, literature, art, custom, convention,
propaganda of all kinds, economic pressure, the food we eat, the climate we live in,
our family, our friends, our experience—every influence you can think of—
and therefore our responses to every problem are conditioned.
Are you aware that you are conditioned?

Krishnamurti

A young bride of the semi-nomadic Mir clan in Gujarat.

You are the product of your environment.
That is why you are not able to see beyond the habits and social conventions
that are rooted deep within you. If you wish to see beyond them,
you must first of all free yourself from the normal way in which you interpret facts.

Svami Prajnanpad

Representation of the sacred cow and other deities.

गावो विश्वस्य मातरः

When one lives with concepts one never learns. The concepts become static.

You may change them but the very transformation of one concept to another is still static, is still fixed.

But to have the sensitivity to feel, seeing that life is not a movement of two separate activities,

the external and the inward, to see that it is one, to realize that the inter-relationship is this movement,

is this ebb and flow of sorrow and pleasure and joy and depression, loneliness and escape,

to perceive nonverbally this life as a whole, not fragmented, nor broken up, is to learn.

Krishnamurti

Scenes of daily life on the ghats of Varanasi where people come to pray, wander about, rest, and wash linen.

My country and your country,

my God and your God—all that is the fragmentation of thought.

Krishnamurti

Offerings to Duraga, near the temple of Sonepur.

We ask ourselves

is it possible to break through this heavy conditioning of centuries immediately

and not enter into another conditioning—to be free,

so that the mind can be altogether new, sensitive,

alive, aware, intense, capable?

Krishnamurti

The nomadic shepherds of Gujarat migrate with their sheep from the north of the country to the south.

One must become poor inwardly

for then there is no seeking, no asking,

no desire—nothing!

It is inward poverty

that can see the truth of a life in which

there is no conflict at all.

Krishnamurti

2,525 kilometers long, the Ganges runs
from the west of the Himalayas to the Gulf of Bengal.

I see these things with an intense joy,

and while I observe, there is no observer, only a beauty almost like love.

For an instant, I am absent, myself and my problems, my anxieties, my troubles: nothing but this wonder exis

Krishnamurti

Sculpture of a Jaïn deity at the temple of Ranakpur.

I have always fought not to project but to be myself.

To retain my own scale, which is a dot, but a vibrating dot, a pulsating dot that is what I'd like to be.

I would like to remain that pulsating dot

which can reach out to the whole world, to the universe.

Chandralekha

The Vishnoïs communities, with a close affinity to nature, are vegetarians and protect trees and animals.

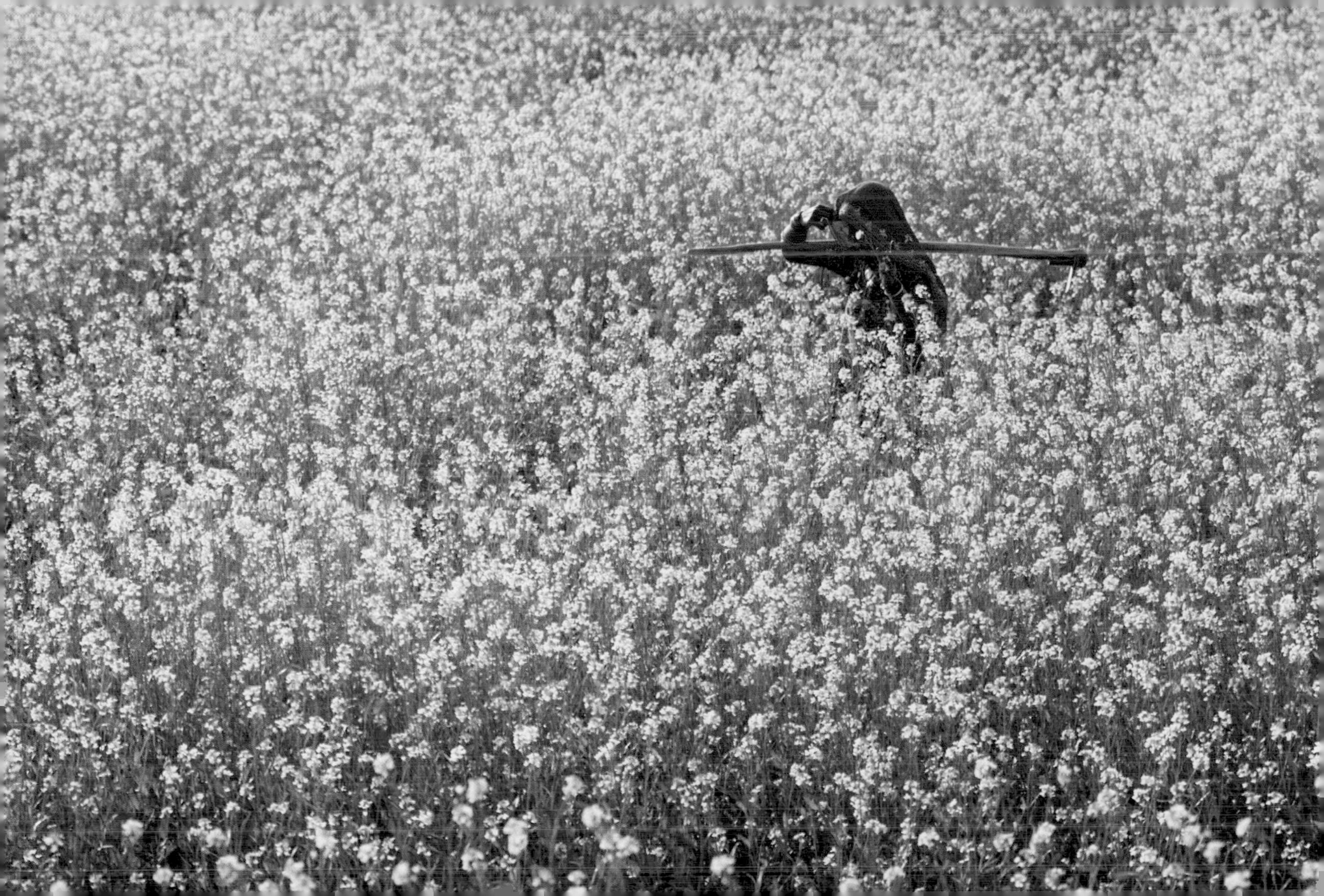

Self is not something as opposed to something else,
it is sunya: we are also all things;
the self represented in all forms, good or bad,
not exclusively or exhaustively in any.

Ramchandra Gandhi

Gita and Lakshmi, two friends from the village of Dasada.

The important question for me is,

is the body a source for creating, for realizing yourself,

for realizing what life is all about? You ask this question

and you go where it takes you and then you ask another question

and then again you follow. So this understanding of the body, of the unity within the body

and the innumerable areas which it reveals to you is what I call realization.

Chandralekha

Classical dance position of Bharat Natyam.

We cross the infinite with every step, and encounter the eternal with every second.

Rabindranath Tagore

The Thar desert.

I have found, yes, I have found the wealth of the divine Name's gem.

My true guru gave me a priceless thing. With his grace, I accepted it.

I found the capital of my several births; I have lost the whole rest of the world.

No one can spend it, no one can steal it. Day by day it increases one and a quarter times.

On the boat of truth, the boatman was my true guru. I came across the ocean of existence.

Mira's Lord is the Mountain Holder, the suave lover, of whom I merrily, merrily sing.

Mira Bai

Neenu, a young dancer of the village of Naneri, in Rajasthan. Following pages: The foothills of the Kanchenjunga, in the north of Sikkim.

22 July

Sensibility is the capacity to feel,
recognize, and distinguish the most tiny and subtle changes.

Svami Prajnanpad

Is there any motion in a straight line? A straight line infinitely projected becomes a circle, it returns to the starting point. You must end where you begin; and as you begin in God, you must go back to God. What remains? Detail work. Through eternity you have to do the detail work.

Swami Vivekananda

A typical floral arrangement of Tamil Nadu.

Civilization, in the real sense of the term, consists not in the multiplication
but in the deliberate and voluntary restriction of the wants.
This alone promotes real happiness and contentment, and increases the capacity for service.
A certain degree of physical harmony and comfort is necessary, but above that level,
it becomes a hindrance instead of a help.
Therefore the ideal of creating an unlimited number of wants and satisfying them
seems to be a delusion and a snare. The satisfaction of one's physical needs, even the intellectual needs
of one's narrow self, must meet at a point a dead stop before it degenerates into physical
and intellectual voluptuousness. A man must arrange his physical and cultural circumstances
so that they may not hinder him in his service of humanity,
on which all his energies should be concentrated.

Mahatma Gandhi

Near the mosque, in central Ujjain, one of the seven sacred cities of Hinduism, an employee of the city prepares the streets for a festival.

In the search for the Truth, for dharma, the real effort does not preclude action
(does not consist in neglecting action), but by trying to accord oneself more and more exactly
with the exterior harmony. The currency of this effort is in becoming:
whatever work you take on, dedicate it to Brahman.

Rabindranath Tagore

Agriculture is the largest employer in India.

No matter how insignificant the thing you have to do,

do it as well as you can,

give it as much of your care and attention as you would give to the thing

you regard as most inportant.

Mahatma Gandhi

Before mealtime, every family makes their bread.

The word duty indicates compulsion.

The word responsibility indicates freedom.

Duties lead one to demand rightfully.

Responsibilities lead one to command respectfully.

Sense of duty is out of attachment.

Sense of responsibility is out of love.

Duties can be thrust upon others.

Responsibilities are taken up by oneself.

There can be unwillingness in performing one's duty.

Responsibility is always taken up willingly.

Maa Purnananda

To water their animals, the villagers of Thar mix milk into the water to cut the salt.

The true source of rights is duty.

If we discharge our duties, rights will not be far to seek.

Mahatma Gandhi

A policeman helps an old woman across a congested intersection in Varanasi.
Following pages: A village woman of Maddhya Pradesh returns to the village with forage for her goats.

It is in the very heart of our activity that we search for our goal.

Rabindranath Tagore

Only the intelligence of love and compassion can solve all problems of life.

Krishnamurti

A grandfather and his grandchild in Gujarat.

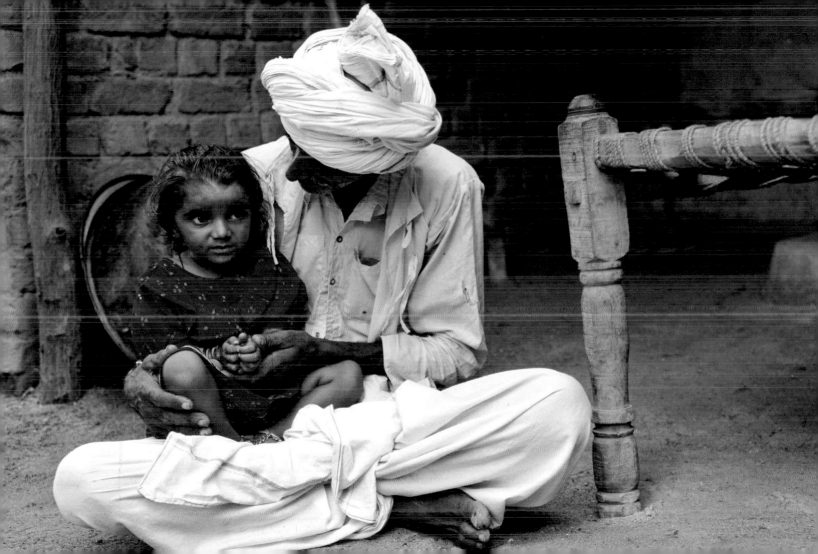

In man, reason quickens and guides the feeling,

in brute, the soul lies forever dormant.

To awaken the heart is to awaken the dormant soul.

— Mahatma Gandhi

Savita, the eldest child, at eight years.

Though there is repulsion enough in Nature, she lives by attraction.

Mutual love enables Nature to persist.

Mahatma Gandhi

Pilgrimage roads, which are traveled on foot, are lined with water dealers.

I am proud to tell you that I belong to a religion in whose sacred language, the Sanskrit, the word exclusion is untranslatable.

Swami Vivekananda

At the Welham School, one of the most reputable of the country, the day begins with a prayer, where all faiths are evoked.

The intellectual aspect is, that love sees and understands.

The emotional aspect is to feel as one with the other person.

Love is unity. There is no "me" in love, only "you."

The behavioral aspect is, that love inspires us to give.

There is no expectation; we do not expect to receive.

Such love is wisdom and liberation in itself.

Svami Prajnanpad

A young mother and her first child at the mela of Sonepur.

What is it exactly that hurts you?
Open your heart and speak. Open your eyes and see.
At the moment that you look with your eyes wide open,
everywhere you will find differences, an infinite variety.

Svami Prajnanpad

The Hunza Valley of Pakistan, famous for its apricots and healthy climate.

Wherever there is a touch of color,
a note of a song, grace in a form,
this is a call to our love.

Rabindranath Tagore

In front of the village mayor,
students of the Kuri school celebrate the day of the Republic.

Love implies generosity, care, not to hurt another,

not to make them feel guilty, to be generous, courteous,

and behave in such a manner that your words and thoughts are born out of compassion.

Krishnamurti

Within the family, the maternal uncle has a vital and effective role.

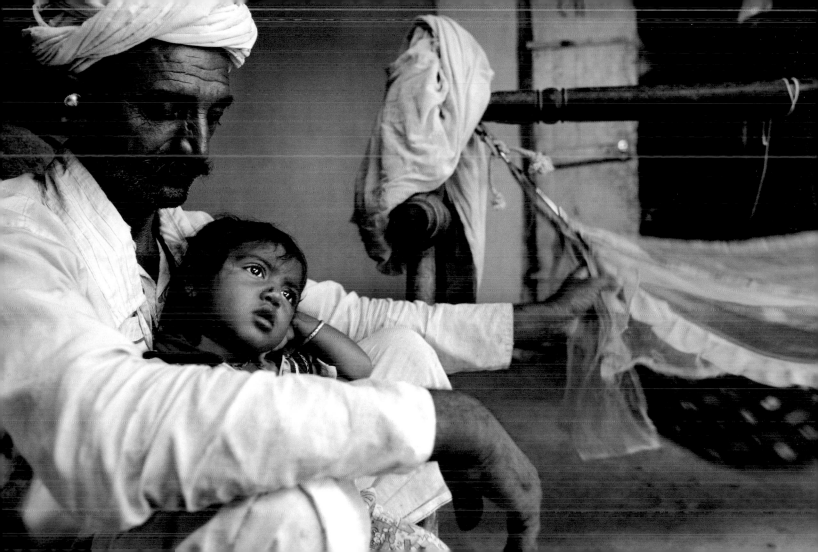

Where do I come from? Where did you find me? asks the baby of his mother.

She weeps and laughs at the same time and, pressing the infant to her breasts, answers,

You were hidden in my heart, darling, you were its desire.

Rabindranath Tagore

Dayalan, nine months old.

Ahimsa means infinite love, which again means infinite capacity for suffering.
Who but woman, the mother of man, shows this capacity in the largest measure?

Mahatma Gandhi

A nomadic shepherdess of Gujarat.

The real ornament of woman is her character, her purity.

Mahatma Gandhi

Prem, a young woman of Adivasi; her name means Love.

If by strength is meant moral power, then woman is immeasurably man's superior.

Has she not greater intuition, is she not more self-sacrificing, has she not greater powers of endurance,

has she not greater courage? Without her man could not be.

If nonviolence is the law of our being, the future is with woman.

Who can make a more affective appeal to the heart than woman?

Mahatma Gandhi

A touch of red worn by a woman shows that she is blessed by marriage.

If only women will forget that they belong to the weaker sex.
I have no doubt that they can do infinitely more than men against war.
Answer for yourselves what your great soldiers and generals would do,
if their wives and daughters and mothers refused to countenance their participation
in militarism in any shape or form.

Mahatma Gandhi

A volunteer teacher with the RIDE Association has the weighty responsibility of helping children of the village escape jobs in textile workshops to attend school.
Following pages: A nearby construction site offers employment to the villagers of Rajasthan, easing the poverty caused by the drought.

12 August

I am firmly of the opinion

that India's salvation depends on the sacrifice and enlightenment of her women.

Mahatma Gandhi

For you, now, meditation involves establishing within yourself
the reality of these two unavoidable rules—difference and change.
Try as hard as possible to convince yourself
that these two rules can neither be changed nor avoided.

Svami Prajnanpad

Inside the surrounding wall of the Temple of Gold, the most sacred site of the Sikhs.

You are unique as you are here and now.

You are never the same. You will never be the same again. You have never before been what you are now.

You will never be it again.

Svami Prajnanpad

Hansi, a cheerful young villager, in the Gujarat.

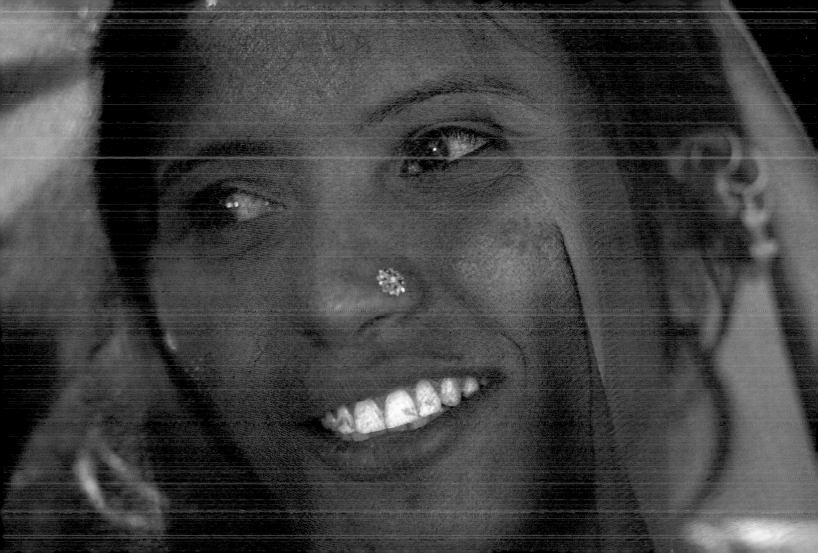

Each one has a special nature peculiar to himself which he must follow and through which he will find his way to freedom.

Swami Vivekananda

A pilgrim in a temple eats a meal served on a banana leaf.

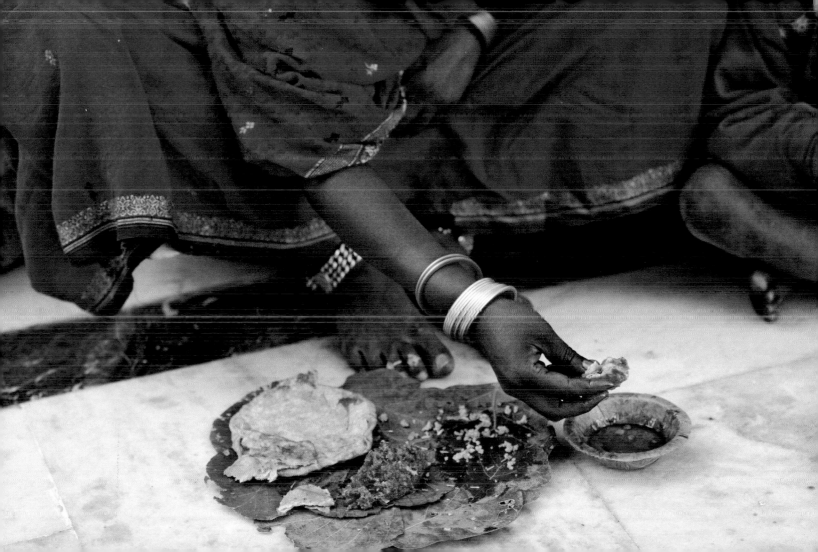

Expansion is life; contraction is death.

Love is life, hatred is death.

We began to die the day we began to contract, to hate others

and nothing can prevent our death,

until we come back to life, to expansion.

Swami Vivekananda

Not all villages in India have their own drinking water.

If you do not think he is different, he is unique, he exists in his own right, there cannot be any relationship.

Svami Prajnanpad

Returning from the pond after a hot day.

When you see that everything is different, that everything is unique,

you become one with the whole.

This is because you no longer judge, compare, or attribute particular characteristics.

Remove the characteristics,

and you no longer have an entity.

Svami Prajnanpad

The full moon, called Karlipumimat, attracts large crowds of pilgrims to all of the sacred places in India.

One person is not another person.

What is he, then? He is unique.

Svami Prajnanpad

Colors are a feminine note in the arid regions of Rajasthan.

To love is to understand and feel that the other person is different.

Svami Prajnanpad

Akash and his father Kulash.

If everybody looked alike, what monotony!

Look alike and think alike-what could we do but sit down and die in despair?

We can't live like a row of chipmunks; variation belongs to human life.

One god, one religion is an old singsong, but there's danger in it.

But, thank God, it can never be.

Swami Vivekananda

A fruit and vegetable stand in Karnataka, which enjoys a tropical climate.

Differentiation, infinitely contradictory, must remain,
but it is not necessary that we should hate each other;
it is not necessary therefore that we should fight each other.

Swami Vivekananda

Religious festivals also allow city dwellers and villagers to enjoy themselves at carnivals.

The golden rule of conduct therefore, is mutual toleration,
seeing that we will never think alike and we shall see the Truth
in fragments and from different angles of vision.
Conscience is not the same thing for all.
While, therefore, it is a good guide for individual conduct,
imposition of that conduct upon all will be an insufferable interference
with everybody's freedom of conscience.

Mahatma Gandhi

The possession of a cow is a sign of prosperity.

We must learn to love those who think exactly opposite to us.

We have humanity for the background, but each must have his own individuality and his own thought.

Push the sects forward and forward till each man and woman are sects unto themselves.

We must learn to love the man who differs from us in opinion.

We must learn that differentiation is the life of thought.

We have one common goal,

and that is the perfection of the human soul, the god within us.

Swami Vivekananda

During the great festival of Pushkar, stalls offer amusement to the villagers come to buy or sell camels.

When the poor come to you in great need, begging for food,

do not harden your hearts against them.

Remember that the poor may once have been rich,

and you may one day be poor.

When you see people who are thin for lack of food,

beg them to accept your help;

remember that you may need their friendship in times to come.

Rig Veda

A mendicant with polio protects himself and his son from the monsoon, in Mumbai; his wheelchair was given to him by a charity.

Variety is the first principle of life.
What makes us formed beings?
Differentiation.
Perfect balance will be destruction.

Swami Vivekananda

Pilgrims take a purifying bath during the full moon, in Sonepur.

In your veins, and in mine, there is only one blood,
The same life that animates us all!
Since one unique mother begat us all,
Where did we learn to divide ourselves?

Kabir

Prayer time in the great mosque of Ahmedabad, under the porch where the names of different prophets are written in calligraphy.

There is no you or me;
all variety is merged into the absolute unity,
the one infinite existence—God.

Swami Vivekananda

After their ritual, a couple return from the sacred water of the Ganges.

Husband and wife merge in each other.

They are one in two or two in one.

Mahatma Gandhi

A sash, the symbol of marriage, joins these newlyweds.

What is a family? It is the place where we feel an atmosphere of love and unity.

And if you can feel this unity in a broader sphere, then gradually your family ties will disappear.

What is the purpose of family life?

It is where we can share emotions however we need to and as freely as possible.

The individual is the one who is cut off, separated.

When you are part of a group,

living for others, you broaden yourself.

This really is family life.

Svami Prajnanpad

A family from Madhya Pradesh returns from the village market.

Meditation can take place when you are sitting in a bus,
or walking in the woods full of light and shadows,
or listening to the singing of the birds,
or looking at the face of your wife or child.

Krishnamurti

Aided by her mother, a dance teacher, Shanti, takes two hours to put on her makeup for a traditional performance of Bharat Natyam.

I believe in the absolute oneness of God and, therefore, humanity.

What though we have many bodies? We have but one soul.

The rays of sun are many through refraction.

But they have the same source.

I cannot, therefore, detach myself from the wickedest soul

nor may I be denied identity with the most virtuous.

Mahatma Gandhi

Rani, fourteen.

2 September

He whom I have searched for has come to meet me,

and he who calls me Other has become me!

Kabir

In the Madhya Pradesh,
a young shepherd returns home after watching over his goats all day.

At one pole of my existence,

I am one with the stones and the tree branches.

Thus, I must submit to the yoke of the universal law.

It is this, in the end, that is the very basis of my life.

And that force comes from that which is closely bound up in the unity of the world,

which is in full communication with all things.

But at the other pole, I am distinct from all of the rest.

Here, I have broken the barriers of equality

and I find myself alone, as an individual.

I am absolutely unique, I am me, I am incomparable.

The whole of the mass of the universe can not crush this individuality that is mine.

I maintain it, despite the formidable gravitation of all that exists.

It is small in appearance, but great in reality.

Rabindranath Tagore

A farmer of the Vishnoi, in Rajasthan, tends to his rape field.

The key to an easy relationship with other people is not to impose your ego, nor to crush the ego of others.

Svami Prajnanpad

The routine of village life allows for moments of relaxation.

Knowledge is the annihilation of the separation between me and the other.

Svami Prajnanpad

Pilgrims from Maharashtra during the great religious festival of Kumbh Mela, which takes place in Nashik every twelve years.

How does seeing the difference permit unity?

Quite simply, because physically speaking there cannot be unity, since the physical plane consists of shapes, and all shapes are different.

Unity only exists in the heart. It is a feeling: love.

And in love the notion of self disappears; only the other remains.

Svami Prajnanpad

At dusk, peacocks and domestic animals drink from the pond of Amballa.

Love can come into being only when there is total self-abandonment.

Krishnamurti

The daily tranquillity of a village in Tamil Nadu.

The infinite oneness of the Soul is the eternal sanction of all morality.

You and I are not only brothers—every literature voicing man's struggle towards freedom

has preached that—but you and I are really one.

This is the dictate of Indian philosophy.

This oneness is the rationale of all ethics and all spirituality.

Swami Vivekananda

Early-morning mist shrouds the Pushkar oasis in the Thar desert.
Following pages: Cranes take to the air, migrating in autumn from Siberia.

An individual is a separate entity without connection.

A person is an individual connected.

Svami Prajnanpad

Why is the lamp extinguished?
I surrounded it with my robe to shelter it from the wind; this is why the lamp is extinguished.

Why has the flower wilted?
I pressed it to my heart with anxiety and love; this is why the flower has wilted.

Why is the river dry?
I built a dike across it so that it would serve me and me alone; this is why the river is dry.

Why is the harp string broken?
I tried to play a note too high for it; this is why the harp string is broken.

Rabindranath Tagore

The symbolic lotus decorates the ponds around temples.

Why is there this division between man and man, between race and race, culture against culture, one series of ideologies set one against another? Why? Why is there this separation?

Krishnamurti

Founded in 1458, the fortress of Kumbhalgash has been stormed only one time in history.
The ancient fortifications, 36 kilometers long, shelter close to 360 temples in the heart of Aravalli.

We are fragmented. We are one person at the office and another at home,
we speak of democracy and are autocrats in our hearts;
we speak of love for our neighbors even as we kill that love with our competitive spirit;
one part of us works, watches, and acts independently of the other.
Are you conscious of the fragmentation of your existence? Is it possible for a mind
that has splintered the structure of its thoughts to perceive the broad field of consciousness?

Krishnamurti

In the cities, small shopkeepers and hurried salesmen take advantage of even the tiniest space.

Two people who have lived together for a long time
have an image of each other which prevents them from really relating to each other.
Therefore, it is important to understand, not intellectually, but actually in your daily life,
how you have built these images about your wife, your husband,
your neighbor, your child, your country, your leaders, your politicians,
your gods—you have nothing but images.
These images create the space between you
and what you observe
and in that space there is conflict.

Krishnamurti

Family planning advertisement: A happy family, two children.

दो बच्चों
के
क्या कहने।
घर आंगन
के
हैं ये गहनें॥

In nature there is fundamental unity running through all the diversity we see about us.

Religions are given to mankind so as to accelerate the process of realization of fundamental unity.

Mahatma Gandhi

Constructed in 1433, the Jain temple of Adinath, in Ranakpur, is one of the jewels of India, with its 420 columns covered in delicate carving.

In the physical world there is an indestructible continuity of relations
between hot and cold, light and darkness, movement and repose,
as well as between the bass and treble notes of a piano.
This is because opposites do not bring confusion to the world; they bring harmony.

Rabindranath Tagore

A winter twilight on the Dal lake of Srinagar, in Kashmir.

The connection of love is total.
In love, difference disappears
and the human soul accomplishes
its object in perfection,
exceeding its own boundaries
and traversing the threshold of infinity.

Rabindranath Tagore

Two students at the Welham School for boys, in Dehra Dun,
one of the country's finest institutions, enjoy recess.

Society cannot be changed unless man changes.

Man, you and others, have created these societies

for generations upon generations.

Krishnamurti

A farmer's cart in the Aravalli mountains.

"If I change, will the world have any value?"

That is a wrong question, if one may point out. It is wrong because you are the rest of humanity.

Krishnamurti

Transplanting of the rice paddies in Tamil Nadu, after the rainy season.

It is not others who must change, but you.

Svami Prajnanpad

The Buddhist site of Ellora, a sixth-century excavation, is one of the most remarkable in Indian history.

As long as individuality survives, that is,
as long as you continue to see others as separate from you,
a feeling of hostility towards them cannot fail to prevail.

Svami Prajnanpad

Constructed in 1650, in the heart of the bazaar of old Delhi, Jama Mashid, where devout Muslims meet at the festival of Id, is the largest mosque in India.

When there is space between you and the object you are observing

you well know there is no love, and without love, however hard you try to reform the world

or bring about a new social order or however much you talk about improvements,

you will only create agony.

So it is up to you.

Krishnamurti

Offerings to the Ganges, in Mirzapur.

Every day we see or read of appalling things happening in the world as the result of violence in man.

You may say, "I can't do anything about it," or "How can I influence the world?"

I think you can tremendously influence the world if you yourself are not violent,

if you lead actually every day a peaceful life—a life which is not competitive, ambitious, envious—

a life which does not create enmity.

Small fires can become ablaze.

Krishnamurti

While on the road, pilgrims must fend for themselves.

Our contribution
to the progress of the world must, therefore,
consist in setting our own house in order.

Mahatma Gandhi

A woman of Madhya Pradesh in the village of Adivasi,

Though they may take various roads, all are on the way.

Swami Vivekananda

Varanasi, the City of Divine Light.

Selfishness in man is a beginning.

Rabindranath Tagore

A mother and child in Gujarat relish a moment of peace in the shade of a tree.

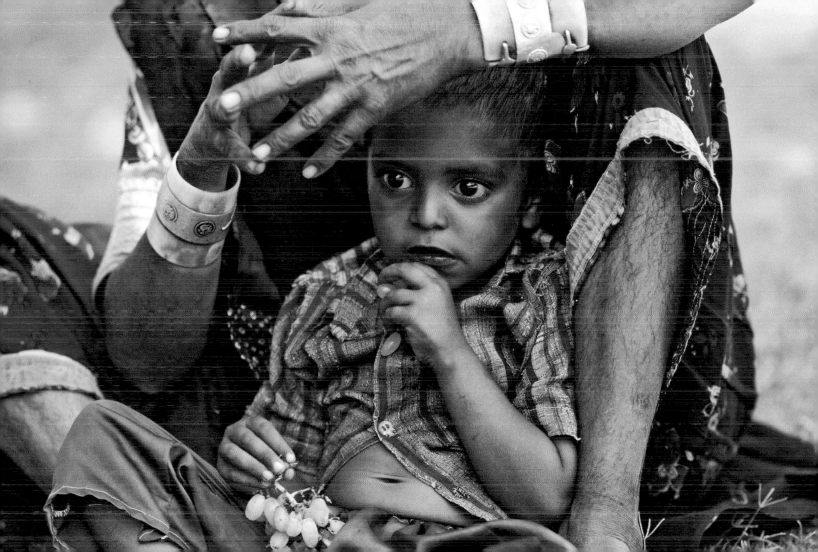

That which is immoral is imperfectly moral,
just as that which is false is true to an inadequate degree.

Rabindranath Tagore

Two porters carry a widow to the summit of the sacred Jain site of Palitana.

We know now that toleration is not sufficient toward another religion; we must accept it.

Thus it is not a question of subtraction, it is a question of addition.

The truth is the result of all these different sides added together.

Each religion represents one side, the fullness being the addition of all these.

Swami Vivekananda

The temple of Shiva and its decorated entrance towers in the village of Tirukalikundram, in Tamil Nadu.

Do not destroy. Iconoclastic reformers do no good to the world.

Help, if you can; if you cannot, fold your hands, stand by, and see things go on.

Therefore say not a word against any man's convictions, so far as they are sincere.

Secondly, take man where he stands, and from thence give him a lift.

Swami Vivekananda

We do not progress from error to truth, but from truth to truth.
Thus we must see that none can be blamed for what they are doing, because they are,
at this time, doing the best they can. We learn only from experience.

Swami Vivekananda

Lakshmi, a child who has recently escaped the textile workshops of Tamil Nadu, thanks to the RIDE Association, discovers the privilege of going to school.

To make a decision is an illusion.

Behind the decision

is the hidden belief

that everyone is the same.

Svami Prajnanpad

After the month of Ramadan, devout Muslims of Delhi press around the door
of the Jama Mashid mosque to celebrate the day of Id.

Man has been steadily progressing towards ahimsa.

Our remote ancestors were cannibals.

Then came a time when they were fed up with cannibalism and they began to live on the chase.

Then came a stage when man was ashamed of leading the life of a wandering hunter.

He therefore took to agriculture and depended principally on mother earth for his food.

Thus from being a nomad he settled down to civilized stable life, founded villages and towns,

and from a member of a family he became a member of a community and a nation.

All these are the signs of progressing towards ahimsa and diminishing violence.

Mahatma Gandhi

On the ghats of Varanasi, a man meditates, facing the Ganges and the rising sun.

For me, nonviolence is not a mere philosophical principle.

It rules my life. It is the rule and breath of my life.

It is a matter not of the intellect but of the heart.

Mahatma Gandhi

It is rare that the operator of a bicycle taxi, quite useful in the congested back streets, owns his own vehicle.

The sum-total of the experience of the sages of the world is available to us
and would be for all time to come.
Moreover, there are not many fundamental truths,
but there is only one fundamental truth which is Truth itself,
otherwise known as nonviolence.

Mahatma Gandhi

At the monastic complex of Sanchi, these sculptures in shallow relief date from the second century B.C.

Nonviolence is the law of our species,

just as violence is the law of the beasts.

In the savage man, the spirit is not awake;

he does not know the other law as he knows that of physical force.

Human dignity demands that one refer to a superior law,

which implements the force of the spirit.

Mahatma Gandhi

Village families prepare chapatis over a cow-dung fire.

Nonviolence and cowardice go ill together.

I can imagine a fully armed man to be at heart a coward.

Possession of arms implies an element of fear, if not cowardice.

But true nonviolence is impossible without the possession of unadulterated fearlessness.

Mahatma Gandhi

A bird stands on a cow at rest.

Nonviolence is not a cloistered virtue to be practiced
by the individual for peace and final salvation,
but it is a rule of conduct for society,
if it is to live consistently with human dignity
and make progress towards the attainment of peace
for which it has been yearning for ages past.

Mahatma Gandhi

Identified with the god Harunam, the monkey is well respected.

Nonviolence is the summit of bravery.

Mahatma Gandhi

Bringing home water, wood, and forage is an important task for village women of India.

Where we suffer we have made it into a personal affair.

We shut out all the suffering of mankind.

Krishnamurti

A man of 102 rests on his traditional rope bed in the family residence, which is shared by five generations.

At the same time, there are millions and millions of boys

in this world dying of starvation—

boys beautiful in body and in mind.

But they are nothing to me. Let them all die.

I am apt to kill them all to save this one rascal to whom I have given birth.

This is what you call love. Not I. Not I.

This is brutality.

Swami Vivekananda

Endangered animals like the elephant and the rhinoceros are protected by law.

Whenever I see an erring man, I say to myself I have also erred;

when I see a lustful man I say to myself, so was I once;

and in this way I feel kinship with everyone in the world

and feel that I cannot be happy without the humblest of us being happy.

Mahatma Gandhi

In the alleyways of old Delhi, a Muslim widow relies on the generosity of the devout at the entrance of the great mosque.

I cannot imagine anything nobler or more national than that for, say, one hour in a day,

we should all do the labor that the poor must do,

and thus identify ourselves with them and through them with all mankind.

Mahatma Gandhi

Rice is the mainstay of southern and eastern India.

Duties to self, to the family, to the country,
and the world are not independent of one another.
One cannot do good to the country
by injuring himself or his family.
Similarly one cannot serve the country
by injuring the world at large.

Mahatma Gandhi

In a village of Maharashtra, a student proudly shows the states of his country.

Give with faith, and never without faith.

Give with dignity. Give with humility. Give with joy.

And give with understanding of the effects of your gift.

Taittiriya Upanishad

Today there are effective treatments for leprosy, which is disappearing.

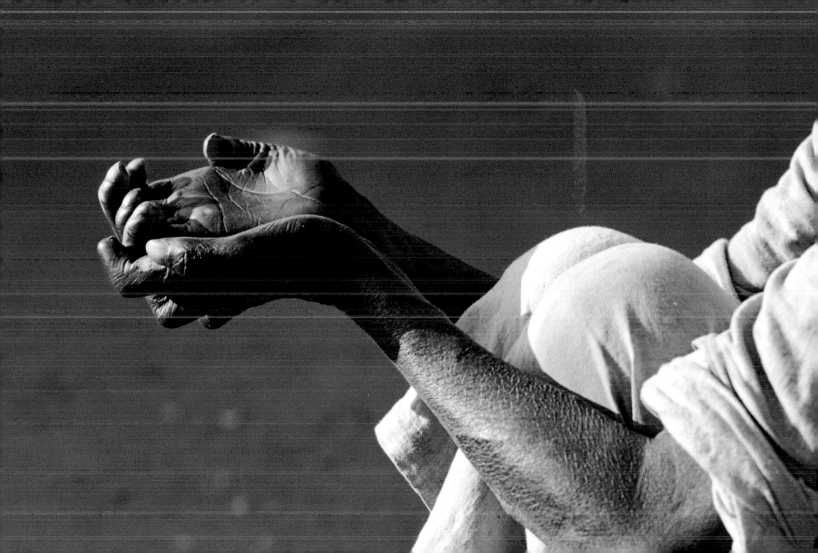

Nations cohere because there is mutual regard among individuals composing them.
Some day we must extend the national law to the universe,
even as we have extended the family law to form nations—a larger family.

Mahatma Gandhi

In Jodhpur, the blue of Brahman houses in old towns has a cooling effect.

When you call yourself an Indian or a Muslim, or a Christian, or a European, or anything else, you are being violent. Do you see why? Because you are separating yourself from the rest of mankind. When you separate yourself by belief, by nationality, by tradition it breeds violence.

Krishnamurti

Boats on the Ganges, transporting sand for the production of cement.

He who seeks to understand violence belongs to no country, no religion, no political party, no particular syste...

What matters to him is the complete understanding of humanity.

According to one school violence is found inside a man;

according to another, it is the result of his social and cultural heritage.

Neither of these viewpoints interests us:

they have no importance; what is important is the way that we are violent,

not the reason for it.

Krishnamurti

The Thar desert.

Facts are not frightening.

But if you try to avoid them, turn your back and run, then that is frightening.

Krishnamurti

Mumbai is a metropolis of dreams, and of despair.

An eye for an eye only ends up making the whole world blind.

Mahatma Gandhi

Constructed in 1459 by the Maharajah of Jodhpur, the fortress is today a museum of the turbulent history of Rajasthan.

I am asking whether it is possible for a human being living psychologically in any society to clear violence from himself inwardly.
If it is, the very process will produce a different way of living in this world.

Krishnamurti

Two friends from Kuri in pleasant conversation, fetching water.

However much I may sympathize with and admire worthy motives,
I am an uncompromising opponent of violent methods even to serve the noblest of causes.

Mahatma Gandhi

Namasté is the common greeting of India.

Nonviolence is the greatest force at the disposal of mankind.

It is mightier than the mightiest weapon of destruction devised by the ingenuity of man.

Mahatma Gandhi

Offerings to the gods.

Better never love,
if that love makes us hate others.

Swami Vivekananda

A baby of Gujarat nestled in his mother's shawl in the shade during the hot season.

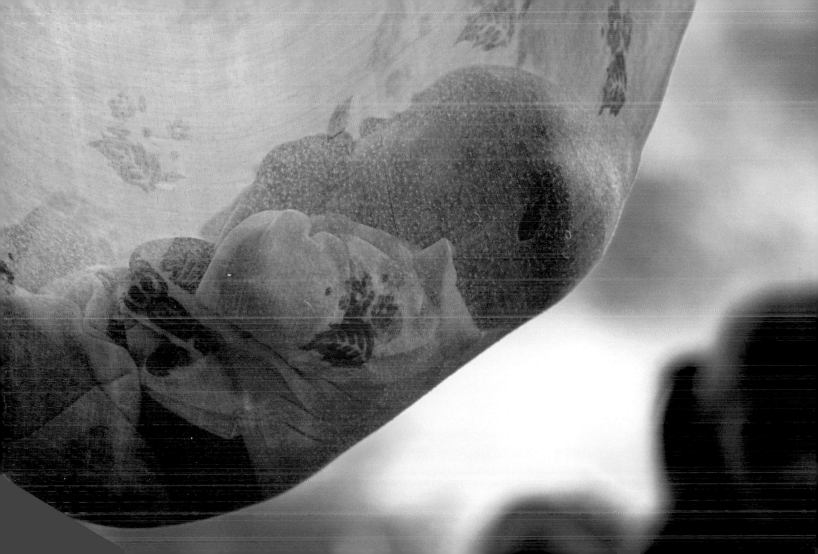

*Until a radical change takes place and we wipe out all nationalities,
all ideologies, all religious division, and establish a global relationship—psychologically and
inwardly first, then organized in the outside world—we shall go on with war.*

Krishnamurti

A young sadhu devoted to the god Shiva on pilgrimage to Trimbak, during the monsoon.

It is man's social nature which distinguishes him from the brute creation.

If it is his privilege to be independent, it is equally his duty to be inter-dependent.

Only an arrogant man will claim to be independent of everybody else and be self-contained.

Mahatma Gandhi

The spirit of brotherhood in Gujarat.

When restraint and courtesy are added to strength, the latter becomes irresistible.

Mahatma Gandhi

A large workforce can be more effective than modern technology on large jobs, such as the building of this railroad.

Do you live and work in the world?

Always act according to the highest moral standards, both in private and in public.

Always be honest in word and deed, both in private and in public.

Master your emotions and control your senses, both in private and in public.

Be calm and patient, both in private and in public.

Take every opportunity to serve others, both in private and in public.

Be kind and gentle to your children, both in private and in public.

Taittiriya Upanishad

The bicycle is the most common form of transportation.

I do not know of any religion apart from human activity.
It provides a moral basis to all other activities which they would otherwise lack,
reducing life to a maze of 'sound and fury signifying nothing.'

Mahatma Gandhi

Garlands are sold as offerings, at the temple of Krishna in Ujjain.

Unity is an intellectual concept.

On an emotional level unity is serenity, equality, and equilibrium.

Svami Prajnanpad

The overcrowded family promotes harmony between brothers, who sleep and play together.
Following pages: Giving food to the poor is a duty for the Buddhist pilgrim who comes to Bodhgaya.

29 October

The noblest moral law
is that we should unremittingly
work for the good of mankind.

Mahatma Gandhi

If the recognized leaders of mankind who have control over the engines of destructions were wholly to renounce their use, with full knowledge of its implications, permanent peace can be obtained. This is clearly impossible without the Great Powers of the earth renouncing their imperialistic design. This again seems impossible without great nations ceasing to believe in soul-destroying competition and to desire to multiply wants and, therefore, increase their material possessions.

Mahatma Gandhi

On Lake Dal in Srinagar, farmers sell their wares at dawn at floating markets, surrounded by lotus.

It is this desire to express himself that leads him to search for riches and power.

But he must understand that to accumulate material wealth is not to find this fulfillment.

What brings him back to himself is the interior light, and not exterior objects.

Rabindranath Tagore

A stall offers copper kitchen utensils.

Non-possession is allied to non-stealing.

Mahatma Gandhi

A rickshaw operator takes a rest after a long trip in the vast tree-lined arteries of New Delhi.

That economics is untrue which ignores or disregards moral values.
The extension of the law of nonviolence in the domain of economics means nothing less
than the introduction of moral values as a factor to be considered with regulating international commerce.

Mahatma Gandhi

The children of the village of Bihar hope to receive a few small coins from pilgrims to Bodhgaya, where the Buddha attained awakening.

Economic equality is the master key to nonviolent independence.

Mahatma Gandhi

Very few farmers have access to a tractor or a water pump.

*I must confess that I do not draw a sharp line
or any distinction between economics and ethics.*

Mahatma Gandhi

A great majority of road workers are paid by the piece.

Every man has an equal right
to the necessities of life,
even as birds and beasts have.

Mahatma Gandhi

According to legend, parokeets are lovers' go-betweens.

The supreme consideration is man.

Mahatma Gandhi

The Jain community respects all living things and, in the ancient temple of Ranakpur, monkeys are pets.

Propaganda can never tell the truth; truth can never be propagated.

Krishnamurti

When you have an ideal will you think it helps rid you of 'what is,' but it never does.
You may preach non-violence for the rest of your life
and all the time be sowing the seeds of violence.

Krishnamurti

*To slight a single human being is to slight those divine powers
and thus harm not only that being but with him the whole world.*

Mahatma Gandhi

It is quite proper to resist and attack a system but,
to resist and attack its author is tantamount to resisting and attacking oneself.
For we are all tarred with the same brush.

Mahatma Gandhi

The end to be sought is human happiness combined with full mental and moral growth.
This end can be achieved under decentralization.
Centralization as a system is inconsistent with a non-violent structure of society.

Mahatma Gandhi

The spirit of democracy
is not a mechanical thing
to be adjusted by abolition of forms.
It requires change of heart.

Mahatma Gandhi

Ten-month-old Abai Kumar and his father.

We say that if a temple, or a symbol, or an image helps you to realize the Divinity within,
you are welcome to it. Have two hundred images if you like.
If certain forms and formulas help you to realize the Divine,
God speed you; have, by all means, whatever forms, and whatever temples,
and whatever ceremonies you want to bring you nearer to God. But do not quarrel about them;
the moment you quarrel, you are not going Godward, you are going backward, towards the brutes.

Swami Vivekananda

The god of literature and music, Ganesh encourages all enterprises.

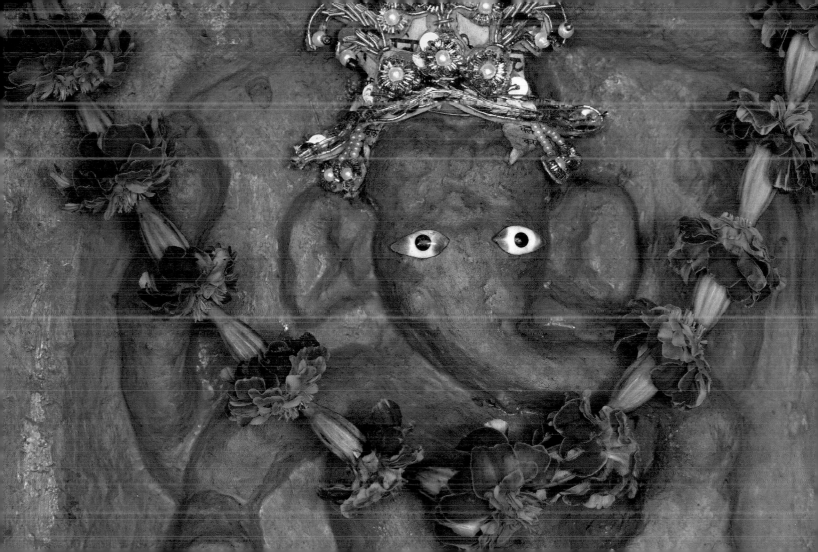

Religion is more than life.

Remember that his own religion is the truest to every man
even if it stands low in the scales of philosophical comparison.

Mahatma Gandhi

A purifying morning bath, in Sonepur.

If all were of the same religious opinion, there would be no religion.

No sooner does a religion start than it breaks into pieces.

The process is for the religion to go on dividing until each man has his own religion,

until each man has thought out his own thoughts

and carved out for himself his own religion.

Swami Vivekananda

On the border with Pakistan in the Thar desert, Danla Khan, 74-year-old patriarch, rests in his room, painted blue to discourage insects.

What then do I mean by the ideal of a universal religion?

I do not mean a universal philosophy, or a universal mythology, or a universal ritual,

but I mean that this world must go on, wheel within wheel.

What can we do?

We can make it run smoothly, we can lessen friction, we can grease the wheels, as it were.

By what?

By recognizing variation.

Just as we have recognized unity, by our very nature so we must also recognize variation.

We must learn that truth may be expressed in a thousand ways, and each one yet be true.

We must learn that the same thing can be viewed from a hundred different standpoints,

and yet be the same thing.

Swami Vivekananda

The Jain community of India gathers every morning to feed 600 kg of grain a day to the cranes that migrate to Khichan every winter.

I make no distinction between one religion and another.

People may worship me in any form they wish.

The form of worship does not matter to me;

my only concern is the quality of love which is expressed in worship.

I accept every kind of worship, because I am supreme.

The Bhagavad Gita

One of the eleven gopurem (porch towers) of the Maduraï sanctuary, decorated with a profusion of statues of gods and characters from Hindu mythology, common in Dravidian art.

If a man reaches the heart of his own religion,
he has reached the heart of the others too.

Mahatma Gandhi

A Muslim ascetic, the Fakir travels all the roads of India, from mosque to mosque.

A profound understanding of religions allows the destruction of the barriers that separate them.

Mahatma Gandhi

A rock painting of the god Shiva transferred to cloth, in the Madhya Pradesh.

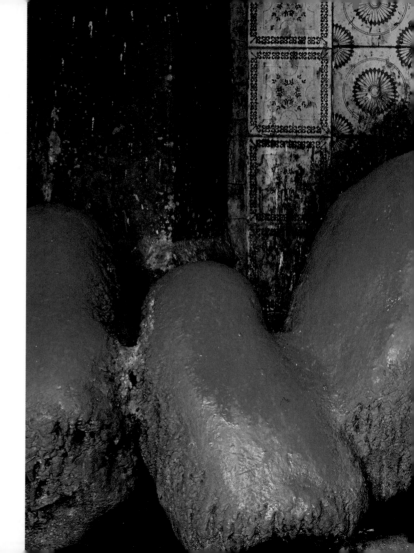

Autumn

The autumn comes, a maiden fair
In slenderness and grace,
With nodding rice-stems in her hair
And lilies in her face.
In flowers of grasses she is clad;
And as she moves along,
birds greet her with their cooing glad
Like bracelets' tinkling song.

Kalidasa

A small temple of white marble, constructed in 1899, in homage to Maharajah Jaswant Singh II of Jodhpur.

Bees suck nectar from many different flowers, and then make honey.

One drop of honey cannot claim to come from one flower, and another drop of honey from another flower,

the honey is a single consistent whole.

In the same way, all beings are one even though they are not aware of this.

The tiger and the lion, the wolf and the boar, the worm and the moth, the gnat and the mosquito,

all come from the soul, and are part of the soul.

Chandogya Upanishad

Petals left by pilgrims as an offering in the bassin of an altar.

Between me and the smallest animal,

the difference is only in manifestation,

but as a principle he is the same as I am,

he is my brother, he has the same soul as I have.

Swami Vivekananda

In the cities, domestic animals scrounge peelings from the streets.

I often ask myself at what point can a man and a beast that cannot talk recognize each other.

From the early paradise, at the dawn of creation, runs the path where their hearts meet.

Although their connection has long been forgotten,

traces of their continuing association has not been erased.

And, suddenly, in a wordless harmony,

a dim memory awakens and the beast looks on the face of the man with tender trust

and the man casts his eyes upon the beast with an amused tenderness.

It is as if two friends, both wearing masks, meet

and vaguely recognize each other through their disguises.

Rabindranath Tagore

Hindus consider the cow to be a member of the family.

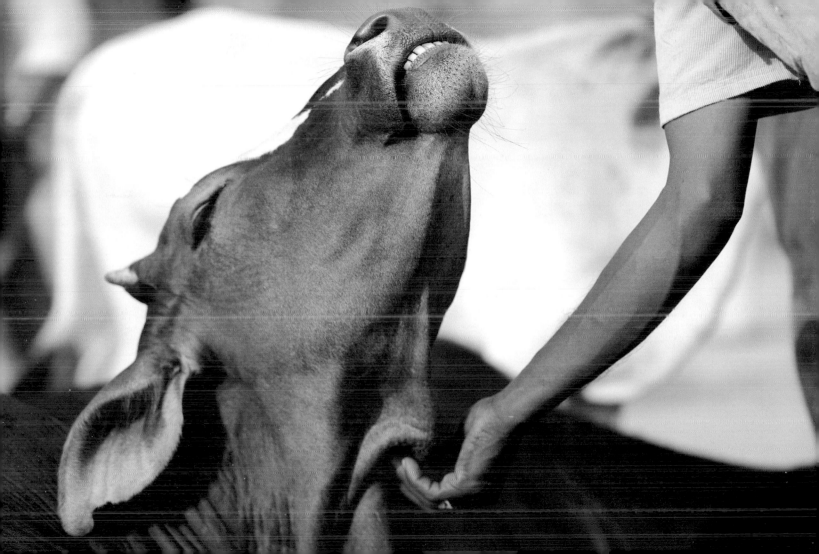

How can you regard yourself as subject and other beings as objects,

when you know that all are one?

Brihadaranyaka Upanishad

In November, the livestock fair of Pushkar draws thousands of farmers.

Water, you are the one that brings us life. You are the source of nourishment that gives us strength.

We rejoice at your existence.

We drink you with joy, as babies drink their mothers' milk.

And when we swallow you, we receive love.

Water, carry away all my sins and my failures, all that has been bad in my life.

I seek you today; I shall plunge into your wetness.

Drown me in splendor.

The Vedas

Pollution is one of the major threats to drinking water. Following pages: An elephant at the temple of Varkala, on the coast of Malabar, facing the Sea of Araby.

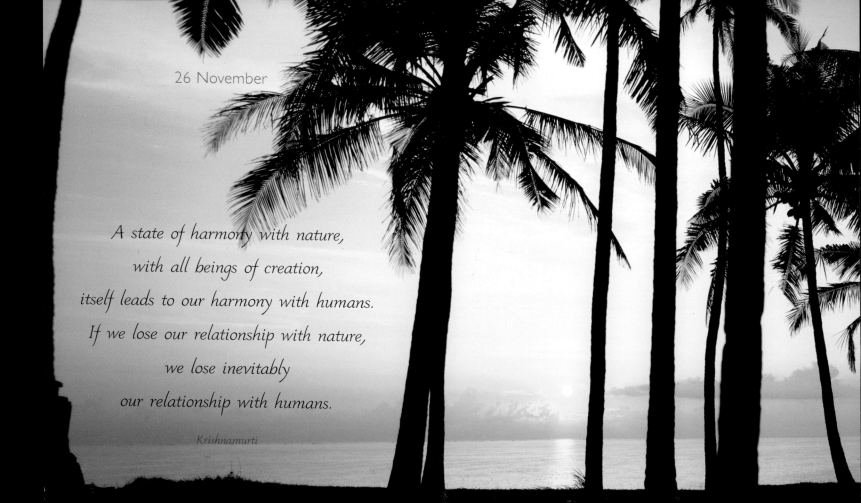

26 November

A state of harmony with nature,
with all beings of creation,
itself leads to our harmony with humans.
If we lose our relationship with nature,
we lose inevitably
our relationship with humans.

Krishnamurti

I have found that life persists in the midst of destruction

and therefore there must be a higher law than that of destruction.

Only under that law would a well-ordered society

be intelligible and live worth living.

And if that is the law of life,

we have to work it out in daily life.

Mahatma Gandhi

A footprint at the Temple of Adinath, the premier prophet of the Jain religion.

Humanity is not divided into airtight compartments
that inhibit going from one to the other.
And when one counts them in the thousands,
they will not be less linked one to the other.

Mahatma Gandhi

A photograph immortalizing a group of villagers standing before a painted wooden ornament in Pushkar, Rajasthan.

We think as our ancestors did, away back in pre-historic ages.
Where even tradition cannot pierce the gloom of that past,
there our glorious ancestors have taken up their side of the problem
and have thrown the challenge to the world.
Our solution is renunciation, giving up, fearlessness, and love;
these are the fittest to survive. Giving up the senses makes a nation survive.

Swami Vivekananda

At the village well in Bodra in the Arawalli mountains.

True civilization does not mean congregating in cities and living a foolish life,
but going Godward, controlling the senses, and thus becoming the ruler in this house of the Self.

Swami Vivekananda

A view of the Citadel at sunset, in the city of Jodhpur.

A civilization must be judged and assessed, not by the level of power it has reached,

but by how it develops and expresses a love of humanity

through its laws and institutions.

The first and last criterion one must submit to is:

Is it recognizable, and to what level, that man is more a spirit than a machine?

Rabindranath Tagore

On an Ahmedabad sidewalk, a public scribe fills out administrative forms.

The world in its essence is the reconciliation of opposite forces.

These forces, like the right hand and left hand of the creator, act in perfect harmony,

and yet in opposite directions

Rabindranath Tagore

The greeting Namasté is made with hands pressed together, recognizing the divine nature of the other.

Your reactions are shared by all humanity.
Your brain is not yours,
it has evolved through centuries of time.
So we are questioning deeply whether there is an
individual at all. We are the whole of humanity,
we are the rest of mankind.

Krishnamurti

The bindi placed between the eyes is a decoration used by many women.

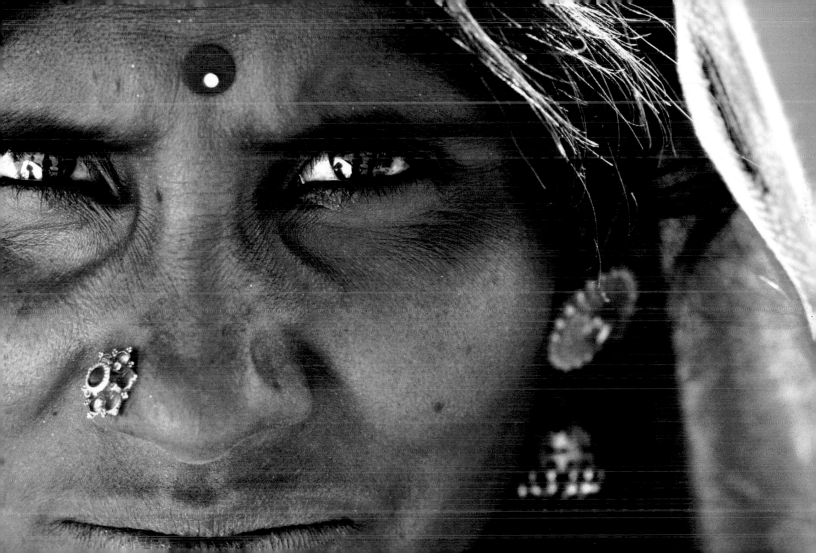

Religion is but one tree with many branches.

If you look only upon the branches, then you are tempted to say that there are many religions;

but if you look at the whole tree, you understand that there is but one religion.

Mahatma Gandhi

The roots of the widespread banyan tree sends up branches to the sun.

Until man can accord to others the right of free belief on all subjects, and be willing to believe truth under whatever form it might appear, no universal religion will be manifest to the world.

Swami Vivekananda

The birth of a first child establishes a woman's position in the home of her in-laws, where she lives after marriage.

If you see God within every man and woman,
then you can never do harm to any man or woman.
If you see God in yourself, then you attain perfection.

The Bhagavad Gita

Shakina, of the Mir clan in Gujarat.

The key to cosmic awareness, to a consciousness of God,

is in the understanding of the soul.

Rabindranath Tagore

Krishna, dancer of Bharat Natyam.

This little earthly horizon of a few feet is not that which bounds the view of our religion.

Ours is beyond, and still beyond, beyond the senses, beyond space,

and beyond time, away, away beyond,

till nothing of this world is left and the universe itself

becomes like a drop in the transcendent ocean of the glory of the soul.

Swami Vivekananda

Jewelry is the only thing of value possessed by the nomadic Mir clan.

The whole universe is to us a writing of the Infinite in the language of the finite.

Swami Vivekananda

At twilight, nature comes to life; the parrots fly in flocks, animals drink in the fading light, silence falls on the villages.

There is one God and He

is the enemy of no one.

Guru Nanak

The Himalayan mountain range in winter—an aerial view of Ladakh, toward the southwest.

It is quite evident that our world is useful and that it provides for our needs,

but our connection to it does not end there.

We are united to it by a connection much larger and more truthful than that of necessity.

Our soul is drawn to it; our love of life is in reality a desire in us to seek our connection with this universe.

And this connection is love.

Rabindranath Tagore

The Mussoorrie region is an idyllic place where newlyweds come to spend their honeymoon.

The fact that there are so many men still alive in the world
shows that it is based not on the force of arms but on the force of truth or love.
Therefore, the greatest and most impeachable evidence of the success of this force
is to be found in the fact that, in spite of all the wars of the world,
it still lives on.

Mahatma Gandhi

The characteristic of my nation is this transcendentalism,
this struggle to go beyond, this daring to tear the veil off the face of nature
and have at any risk, at any price,
a glimpse of the beyond.

Swami Vivekananda

A wonder of the world built in 1648, the Taj Mahal was constructed by the Moghul emperor Shah Jahan, in homage to his favorite wife.

When water joins with water, it is not a meeting but a unification.

Svami Prajnanpad

The Himalayas provide water to the north of India, and bring devastation during the monsoons.

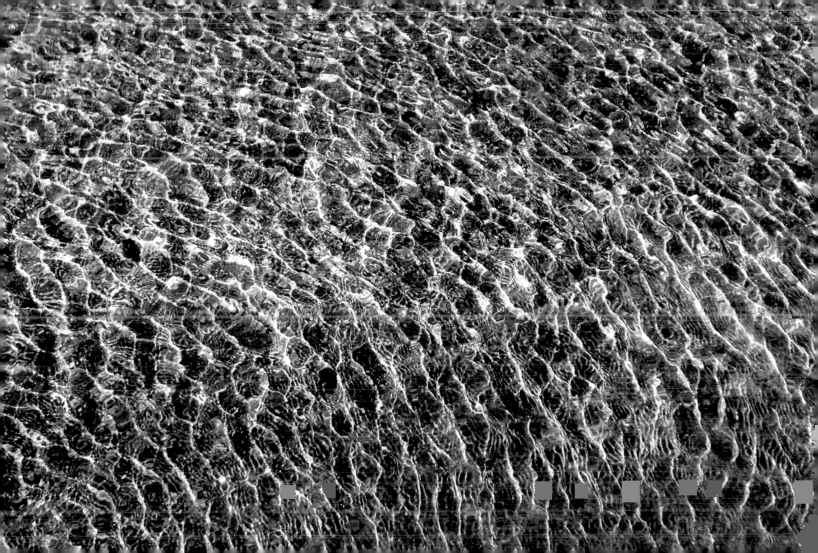

In his essence, man is not a slave to himself, nor to the world; he is a lover.

His freedom and accomplishments are in love,

which is another name for perfect understanding.

In this ability to understand, in this impregnation of everything that is,

he is one with the Spirit that penetrates everything,

and that is also the breath of the soul.

Rabindranath Tagore

A significant number of Rajasthan villagers emigrate to find work because of the recurring drought.

To reach cosmic understanding,

it is necessary to unite our feeling with that infinite feeling that penetrates everything.

In fact, for man, true progress coincides with the breadth of the base of our feelings.

All our poetry, philosophy, science, art, and religion

serve to embrace with our understanding

the spheres too vast and high.

Rabindranath Tagore

In Ahmedabad, the room of a priest of the great mosque Jama Mashid, constructed in 1423, with its 260 columns.
Following pages: The villagers of Kuri meet at the pond to draw water and let their beasts drink.

It is only a mind that looks at a tree or the stars or the sparkling waters of a river

with complete abandonment that knows what beauty is,

and when we are actually seeing we are in a state of love.

Krishnamurti

This is a good point to understand that the sum and substance of this lecture is that there is but One Existence, and that One Existence seen through different constitutions appears either as the earth, or heaven, or hell, or gods, or ghosts, or men, or demons, or world, or all these things.

Swami Vivekananda

Offering on the Ganges in a cupola made with the leaves of the sacred Pipal tree.

Truth is that which one wishes in its totality. Have you reached it?

Krishnamurti

The coast of Malabar and the Sea of Araby, in Kerala.

The saffron of virtue and contentment

Is dissolved in the water gun of love and affection.

Pink and red clouds of emotion are flying about,

Limitless colors raining down.

All the covers of the earthen vessel of my body are wide open;

I have thrown away all shame before the world.

Mira's Lord is the Mountain Holder, the suave lover.

I sacrifice myself in devotion to His lotus feet.

Mira Bai

A young dancer rests during a folklore performance.

Within, everything is connected.

This is because an action in one part produces a similar reaction elsewhere

and thus a response.

Svami Prajnanpad

A cenotaph of the Maharajahs of Jaisalmer, in the Thar desert.

Oh, if you only knew yourselves! You are souls; you are gods.
If ever I feel [that I am] blaspheming, it is when I call you man.

Swami Vivekananda

Amidst this chaos there is harmony, throughout these discordant sounds there is a note of concord; and he who is prepared to listen to it will catch the tone.

Swami Vivekananda

A typical gesture of Bharat Natyam, a classical dance of Tamil Nadu.

We encounter this surprising paradox between us:
the Whole appears as a multitude,
the appearance is opposite to the truth,
and yet it is inseparably linked.

Rabindranath Tagore

The lighting of Parliament, during the celebration of Independence Day.

But if you are not connected with all living beings on earth,

you risk losing your relationship with humanity, with human beings.

We never truly look at a tree's qualities; we never touch it to feel how solid it is, how rough its bark is,

to listen to the sound it makes. Not the sound of the wind in the leaves,

nor the morning breeze that makes them rustle, but its own sound, the sound of the trunk,

the silent sound of the roots. You have to be extremely sensitive to hear this sound.

It is not the noise people make, the chattering of thoughts, nor that of human quarrels and wars,

but the very sound of the universe.

Krishnamurti

Twilight is always enlivened by the joyful song of parrots.

When the life of a man, freed from all distractions, finds its unity in the spirit,

the knowledge of the infinite comes to him immediately and naturally,

like light from a flame.

Rabindranath Tagore

Flight of the cranes, at twilight, in Khichan.

Meditation is to be aware of every thought and of every feeling,
never to say it is right or wrong, but just to watch it and move with it.
In that watching you begin to understand the whole movement of thought and feeling.
And out of this awareness comes silence.

Krishnamurti

Beginning of a yoga sequence, facing the Sea of Araby.

Silence is a great benediction, it cleanses the brain, gives vitality to it,
and this silence builds up great energy, not the energy of thought or the energy of machines,
but unpolluted energy, untouched by thought.
It is the energy that has incalculable capacity, skills.
And this is a place where the brain, being very active, can be silent.
That very intense activity of the brain has the quality and the depth
and the beauty of silence.

Krishnamurti

Fishermen on the Ganges, in the calm of twilight.

The soul is the home of all living beings;

and from the soul all living beings derive their strength.

There is nothing in the universe that does not come from the soul.

The soul dwells within all that exists;

it is the truth of all that exists.

You, my son, are the soul.

Chandogya Upanishad

At 6,000 meters, the summit of Kang Tokal in Nepal dominates the Buddhist valleys of Dolpo, to the north, and the Hindu valleys in the foothills of the Himalayas to the south.

In music, I am the melody.

The Bhagavad Gita

Offerings on the Ganges.

To find God, you must welcome everything.

Rabindranath Tagore

A dance to the gods.

Biographies

Danielle and Olivier Föllmi are the authors of *Offerings: Buddhist Wisdom for Every Day*, *Buddhist Himalayas* (edited in collaboration with Matthieu Ricard), as well as about fifteen photographic works on the Himalayas. Olivier Föllmi, who is French Swiss, lived for many years in the Himalayan valley. After growing up in Latin America, Danielle studied medicine in Paris and completed her degree in anesthesiology in Geneva. She has trained in Europe and in Asia. Their children were born in Tibet. Danielle and Olivier Föllmi travel all over the world to work as part of their project *Offrandes de l'Humanité*, in order to promote the variety of humanity's ideas. Fluent in Hindi, they have a love affair with India, where they have lived for many years.

Giuliano Boccali is professor of Indian studies at the University of Milan, Italy. He has devoted himself to the ancient literature of India, in particular to the classical poetry of nature and love, and has translated many of its masterpieces into Italian.

Author and journalist **Radhika Jha** is a contributor to the *Hindustan Times*. Her novel *Smell* (2000) has been translated into fourteen languages. A professional dancer of classical Odissi as well, Radhika Jha has done a number of productions in India and Great Britain. A native of southern India on her mother's side and of the north on her father's, she lives and works in Delhi.

Jean Sellier is a geographer and historian. He is the author of a series of atlases of people published by Editions La Découverte in Paris.

* * * * * * * * * * * * * * *

A scholar of Sanskrit and Indian studies, **Muthusamy Varadarajan** is a member of the Indian Commission for Minorities and director of the National Museum of Delhi. A member of the administrative services for forty years, he occupied important governmental posts, both in India and abroad. An economist and lawyer by education, he maintains a great interest in philosophy, history of religions, theater, plastic arts, architecture, and design, with a particular attention to cultural studies. A great humanist, he has tried hard to discover the truth inherent in all religion and mystical searches, reintroducing the idea of a brotherhood of humanity that transcends all geographical, historic, religious, or ethnic divisions.

Mata Amritanandamayi was born in southern India in 1953. This saint, who embraces every individual, is also known as Amma, and has been given the name Sudhamani, "Jewel of Ambrosia Perfume." A brilliant student, Mata Amritanandamayi was nevertheless forced to quit school upon the death of her mother in order to take care of her family—heavy work for the elder sister of seven small children, who needed to be fed and dressed. Today, more than thirty books, published in more than twenty languages, tell her story. She has given numerous lectures during religious summits at the United Nations in New York in 2000 and in Geneva in 2002.

The **Bhagavad Gita** (400–300 B.C.), "The Song of the Lord," is one of the poems that make up the long epic narrative of the Mahabharata. It recounts the exchange between the hero Arjuna and his charioteer, the god Krishna, on the day before a great battle. Its major theme, yoga, is here presented as a means of attaining "freedom" and union with the divine.

The prince Gautama was born around 2,500 B.C. in the forest of Lumbini, which today is in Nepal. This Indian sage lived to be eighty years old. At thirty-five, the prince achieved his Awakening while sitting under the Tree of Illumination, after having meditated for forty-nine days. He then achieved higher and higher levels of consciousness. Possessing henceforth the Four Noble Truths and the Noble Eight-Fold Path, he became the **Buddha**, that is, the Awakened. Up to the end of his life, he dispensed his doctrine and he transmitted his major teaching, *The Sutra of the Lotus in Eighty Chapters*. His principal teachings were written down between the first century B.C. and the second century A.D.

The celebrated dancer of the 1950s **Chandralekha**, studied first with an illustrious professor of Bharatnatyam, the guru Kancheepuram Ellappa Pillai. Her reinterpretation of the classical traditions of dance and her development of unique sequences of movement made her a well-known choreographer and dancer. Her success continued across the world, where her productions, profoundly iconoclastic and possessed of a great sensuality, captivated a large public. According to Chandralekha, dance is neither a devotion to a divinity nor a sacred tradition; it is above all an impassioned expression of oneself and of all that relates to the earth, eroticism, and the most primitive elements.

Mahatma Gandhi was born in 1869 on the west coast of India. In 1887 he traveled to London to study law, French, Latin, and the sciences. He also read the Bible as well as works of theosophy, and was greatly impressed by the similarities that he perceived between the Sermon on the Mount and the Bhagavad Gita. Upon becoming a lawyer, he left for South Africa, where he fought against racial segregation. Returning to India, Gandhi campaigned for independence through nonviolence and civil disobedience. Living life by his convictions, he has become the supreme example of the annihilation of the ego. Albert Einstein said of him, "Generations to come will have a hard time believing that such a man, of flesh and blood, had come to this earth." He was assassinated on January 30, 1948.

Professor **Ramchandra Gandhi** is a doctor in philosophy, and a graduate of Delhi and Oxford. He has taught in India, Great Britain, and the United States. The author of numerous works, including *The Availability of Religious Ideas*, he has also written and produced several films and plays about Mahatma Gandhi, his grandfather.

Though the birth of **Kabir** is shrouded in mystery, it is nevertheless believed that he came to the earth around 1440 A.D. and that he grew up in a family of Muslim weavers. His religious precepts are of great simplicity. For Kabir, all life is a simple interlude between two spiritual principles, the one being the personal soul, the other, God. For him, salvation depended upon the union between these two divine principles. His philosophy synthe-

sizes Hindi and Muslim concepts. From Hinduism, he took the notion of reincarnation and of the law of Karma. From Islam, he integrated the affirmation of one unique god and the rejection of idolatry and the caste system. He is the author of numerous poems and songs.

We know little of the life of **Kalidasa**, but scholars generally believe that he lived during the reign of Candra Gupta II (c. 380–415 A.D.). According to legend, the poet, who possessed great beauty, received no education. It is said that he was called to aid the goddess Kali, who then gave him great intelligence. Kalidasa is the author of numerous satirical plays—notably *Vikramorvashe*—of great poetic beauty and of humor brimming with imagination, foreshadowing the themes of William Shakespeare's *Midsummer Night's Dream*. Kalidasa's plays enjoy great success to this day.

Born in Mandanapalle, in the southern part of India, on May 12, 1895, **Jiddu Krishnamurti** experienced spiritual awakening in 1925 while on his way to India from the United States. For over sixty years he gave many lectures throughout the world. His major teaching is found in the phrase, "To change society and make it so that peace will reign over the world, you must begin by changing your heart and your thoughts, at the individual level." He died at the age of ninety, on February 17, 1986, in Ojai, California. Today he is considered as one of the great thinkers of our times.

Acharya Mahaprajna was born in 1921, in the small village of Rajasthan. A monk at the age of ten, he later became a great scholar of Jaïns Agamas, the celebrated critic of Indian and Western philosophies. In striving to coordinate the sciences with spirituality, he has acquired a great deal of knowledge, and has authored more than a hundred and fifty books on yoga, religion, and literature. A great specialist in meditation, he is originally a follower of Preksha Dhyan, the meditation technique of the Jaïns.

Sri Ramana Maharshi (1879—1950) left southern India at a very young age to go to Tiruvannamalai, not far from Madras. Apparently without preparation, he chose to develop his devotion to the spirit of renunciation, the essence of all saintly life. He immersed himself in humility, softness, submission, and other virtues. For sixteen years, he lived in the Virupaksa Cave, before moving to Skandasramam (1916–1922), where many people came to see him. After years of sadhana, he attained the understanding of ultimate reality. If Sri Ramana Maharshi, the sage of the holy hill Arunachala, essentially teaches us to follow silence, he nevertheless was successful at transmitting his knowledge.

Mira Bai was born into a noble family of the Rajput warrior clan at the end of the fifteenth century A.D. According to legend, as a child Mira Bai became consumed with the love of Krishna and dedicated her entire life to him. She composes love poems full of devotion that remain, even today, among the most beautiful in the Hindu language.

In the sixteenth century, the guru **Nanak**, son of a Hindu tax collector in Pendjab, in the northwest of India, sought at a very young age the companionship of itinerant ascetics. A professor, his teaching was influenced by the mystic Sufism of Islam and by the devotion, through yoga, to Hinduism. The hymns he composed are concerned with Sikh worship and spirituality.

Patanjali (c. third century B.C.) is the author of the supreme instructions for meditation—the Sutra—that elucidates the yoga of knowledge, as it is defined in the Bhagavad Gita.

Brahman, student, and brought up as a strict orthodox Hindu, **Svami Prajnanpad** (1891-1974) demonstrated while quite young a lively and curious spirit. Graduating with a degree in physics, he taught in colleges before joining the movement of civil disobedience founded by Gandhi. He then took a vow of poverty. He met his master Niralamba Swami in 1921. After a little more than a year as professor in English literature, Indian philosophy, and physics at the celebrated Kashi Vidyapith in Benares, he discovered among the volumes of the school's library the thoughts of Freud—a revelation for someone searching for a connection between daily life and the Upanishads. He saw psychoanalysis as the missing link, the means to assure passage between the narrow and individual conscience imprisoned in the ego and the wider consciousness spoken of in the Upanishads.

Maa Purnananda was born into a large Indian family of powerful businessmen and great yogis. Inspired by the great Bengali mystic of the nineteenth century, Ramakrishna, she decided to leave her family and go to the forest, where she began sadhana, in Assam, at the foot of the Himalayas. There she sought strict communion with God, for hours and days, without interruption, and became known as the goddess of the mountain. Maa Purnananda has devoted her life to the service of humanity, by the transmission of her knowledge of Vedantism, and has helped men and women to become productive citizens of the world. In June of 2002 she created an enterprise in Delhi, with the principal goal of lifting society by nourishing the moral and ethical values. She directs management workshops, seminars, and camps for professionals.

The Reverend **Parthasarathi Rajagopalachari** was born in 1927 in the north of Tamil Nadu. He lost his mother at five and from then on followed his father, who worked for the railroads, into different regions of India. Several years later, he left school and found employment in the chemical industry. At the age of eighteen, he attended a lecture on the Bhagavad Gita, where his spiritual aspirations were awakened. He decided at thirty to study the Hindu religion through the traditional Vaishnava. Seven years later he encountered his master, Shri Ram Chandra of Shahjahanpur, and began to practice Sahaj Marg. Since that time, his whole life has been dedicated to the spiritual cause of service to others. He presently organizes numerous lectures and teaches Sahaj Marg meditation throughout the world.

Head of the state of Tibet, **His Holiness the XIVth Dalai Lama Tenzin Gyatso** is also the spiritual master of his people. Born on July 6, 1935, in a small village in the northeast of Tibet, his holiness was recognized at the age of two as the reincarnation of the XIIIth Dalaï Lama and as an incarnation of Avalokiteshvara, the Buddha of compassion. Enthroned doctor of Buddhist philosophy in 1940 in Lhasa, he agreed to leave Tibet and to go to India following the occupation of his country by the Chinese. Since moving to Dharamsala, he has never ceased to plead for a negotiable solution to the question of Tibet's rulership. In 1989 he received the Nobel Peace Prize for his nonviolent resistance.

After earning renown as a journalist, **Gopal Singh** became a great Sikh scholar. Celebrated also for his poetry, short stories, and literary criticism, he is the author of numerous works, including *Sri Guru Granth Sahib, History of the Sikh People (from 1469 to 1978)*, and *The Religion of the Sikhs*. He was governor of two Indian states after independence.

Rabindranath Tagore (1861-1941) received a private education before leaving, at age seventeen, to study in England. He participated in the Indian nationalist movement in a personal and visionary way; Gandhi was one of his close friends. He rapidly won great success as an author in his native Bengal. He has written novels, poems, musicals, ballets, essays on every genre, and travel journals. A talented musician and painter, he has also left numerous drawings and paintings, as well as songs, of which he composed the music. In 1913, he received the Nobel Prize in Literature for *Gitanjali (Song Offerings)*.

The word *upanishad* means "to sit near to," and refers to groups of pupils sitting near the teacher to learn from him. Written between 800 and 400 B.C., the **Upanishads** are Indian texts on which the Vedic philosophy is based. A compilation of various explications of the Vedas written by disciples, in an epoch when Buddha was spreading his spirituality across India, it constitutes the oldest philosophical writing. Borrowing totally from mysticism, it in no way forms a strict doctrine of a religion.

Valluvar, as the name suggests, was a weaver, and the author of action yoga—a practice of meditation defined in the Bhagavad Gita. He probably lived in the fifth century.

The **Vedas** are the oldest Hindi texts. They have deeply influenced Buddhism, Janism, and Sikh doctrine. They were written over many centuries, beginning in 1200 B.C. The first, the Rig Veda, assembles more than a thousand hymns and prayers written to be chanted.

During the thirty nine years of his short life, **Swami Vivekananda** (1863-1902) wrote four treatises on Hindu philosophy, which have become great classics: *The Jhana Yoga, Bhakti Yoga, Karma Yoga,* and *Raja Yoga*. A poet, he also served as a spiritual guide to all who came to see him for counsel. Swami Vivekananda described himself as "a summary of India." Romain Rolland has said of him, "His words are great music, phrases in the style of Beethoven, stirring rhythms like the march of a Händel chorus. I cannot approach his writing, scattered across the pages of his books, even after thirty years, without feeling shivers throughout my body like electric shocks. And what shocks one must feel when these words come directly from the lips of such a hero!"

Wisdom: 365 Thoughts from Indian Masters and the project *Offrandes de l'Humanité*
were initiated and realized due to the generosity of

an anonymous donor

Lotus & Yves MAHÉ

and with the support of

FUJIFILM
and
in Paris, the **DUPON** laboratories,

which emphasizes their recognition
of the value of humanism
developed in these projects.

*T*ranslated into seven languages, this book is the fruit of a rich and harmonious collaboration:

First the project was carefully prepared by editor Hervé de la Martinière with the help of Bernard Gachet and Olivier Föllmi, who photographed in India for eight months, aided by his two Indian assistants Anna Sirseth and Ngawang Tashi.
It was supported in New Delhi by:
Mr. Dominique Girard, ambassador of France in India, and by
Mrs. Sheila Dixit, minister of head of state of Delhi,
Mr. Jean-Claude Tribolet and Mr. Jérôme Neutres, cultural attachés to the French embassy in India,
Mr. Dileep Padgaonkar,
Mr. J-L. Calmettes, director of Air France in New Delhi,
Mr. Rajiv & Indra Kaul-Artou Voyages in New Delhi,
Mr. Muzahid Malik, specialist of Gujarat.

In France, it was handled in the Föllmi studio by:
Anne-Marie Meneux, his assistant,
Marie-Christine De Sa, his assistant of photography,
Chantal Dubois,
Céline Viala,
Gil Dumas.

The literature team and Danielle Föllmi were responsible for the gathering of the texts and of their selection under the supervision of Mr. Muthusamy Varadarajan, with the aid of Mr. Vidyanivas Mishra, scholar of Sanskrit at the University of Bénarès, and professor Vagish Shukla at IIT in New Delhi.

The book was produced by Éditions de La Martinière in Paris with the support of:
Carole Daprey, Juliette de Trégomain, Emmanuelle Lallemand, Dominique Escartin.

The calligraphy was done by Sophie Verbeek.

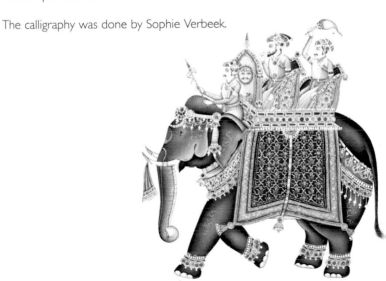

Sources

Archarya Mahaprajna, *You Can Change the World,* Vol. I No. 4 Feb. 2003, Vol. I No 6 April 2003: 12 March; 10, 14, and 15 May.

Buddha, *Kabîr: le fils de Ram et d'Allah.* Paris, © Les Deux Océans, 1988: 13 April.

Chandralekha, *Mirrors and Gestures: Conversations with Women Dancers,* Lakshmi, C.S. New-Delhi, © Kali for Women, 2003: 17 and 19 July.

Gandhi, Mahatma, *All Men Are Brothers, Autobiographical Reflections,* The Continuum Publishing Company, © 2002: 24 January; 26 March; 10 April; 7, 20, 23, 25, 27, and 28 May; 3, 4, 9, 13, 16, and 24 June; 24, 26, 28, and 31 July; 1, 8, 10, 11, 12, and 23 August; 1 and 23 September; 1, 2, 3, 4, 5, 6, 7, 11, 12, 14, 27, 29, and 30 October; 1, 2, 3, 4, 5, 6, 9, 10, 11, 18, 19, 27, and 28 November; 4 and 12 December. *Quotes of Gandhi,* compiled by Shalu Bhalla. Pondichéry, © 1993 Navajwan Trust, Ahmedabad; 29 January; 7 February; 12 April; 4, 24, 26, and 30 May; 1, 11, 23 June; 9 and 29 August; 14 September; 10, 18, 20, 21, 24, and 25 October; 12 and 14 November.

Gopal Singh, *Sri Guru Granth Sahib.* Calcutta, © Birla Foundation: 31 May.

His Holiness the XIVth Dalai Lama, *The Heart of Compassion.* Delhi, © Full Circle, 1997: 11 May.

Kabir, *Cent huit perles éditions.* Paris, © Les Deux Océans, 1995: 21 June. *Au cabaret de l'amour, paroles de Kabir.* Paris, © Éditions Gallimard/UNESCO, 1986: 20 January; 2 September. *Kabîr: le fils de Ram et d'Allah.* Paris, © Les Deux Océans, 1988: 22 January; 27 August. *Sâdhana, Rabindranath Tagore,* Paris © Éditions Albin Michel, 1971: 9 May.

Kalidasa: 20 November.

Krishnamurti, *Freedom From the Known,* Edited by Mary Lutyens © 1969 by Krishnamurti Foundation Trust Limited, UK: 12, 26, and 27 January; 13, 21, 22, 23, and 28 February; 5, 9, 13, 14, 16, 19, 21, 22, 24, 30, 31 March; 1, 9, 17, 19 April; 6, 18, 19, 27 June; 3, 4, 5, 8, 9, 10, 12, 13, 14, 15, and 16 July; 31 August; 7, 12, 13, 21, and 22 September; 15, 16, and 19 October; 8 November; 17, 19, and 27 December. *Krishnamurti to Himself: His Last Journal,* © 1987, by Krishnamurti Foundation Trust Limited, UK: 5, 16, and 30 January; 12 February; 20 and 30 April; 3 and 21 May; 12, 25, 26, and 29 June; 12 and 30 July; 6 August; 11, 17, and 18 September; 8, 17, and 23 October; 7 and 26 November; 3, 25, and 28 December.

Maa Purnananda, *You Can Change the World,* Vol. I, No. 2, December 2002: 27 July.

Mata Amritanandamayi, *You Can Change the World,* Vol. I, No. 3, January 2003: 29 March.

Mira Bai, *Yoga de la dévotion* (Association): 21 July; 20 December.

Guru Nanak, *The Sikh Religion:* Vol. I and 2, Macauliffe Max Delhi © S. Chand & Co. 1963: 10 December.

Nisargadatta, *Kabîr: le fils de Ram et d'Allah. Paris,* © Les Deux Océans, 1988: 22 May.

Patanjali, *366 Reading Series.* Bombay, © Jaico Publishing, 2003: 8 March.

Rabindranath Tagore, *Sâdhana, Paris,* © Éditions Albin Michel, 1971: 9, 18, 23, 25, 28, and 31 January; 1, 2, 11, and 16 February; 3 March; 2, 5, 6, 7, 14, 25, 28, and 29 April; 1, 5, 12, 13, 19, and 29 May; 2 and 5 June; 1, 20, 25, and 29 July; 5 August; 3, 15, 16, 25, and 26 September; 31 October; 1, 2, 7, 11, 15, 16, 24, 26, and 31 December. *Le jardinier d'amour: la jeune lune.* Paris, © Éditions Gallimard, 1964: 7 August; 10 September; 23 November; 7 December.

Rev. Parthasarathi Rajagopalachari, *You Can Change the World,* Vol. I, No. 4, February 2003: 19 January.

Svami Prajnanpad, *ABC d'une sagesse,* Paroles choisies par Daniel Roumanoff. Paris, © Éditions La Table Ronde, 1998: 4 and 17 January; 8, 9, 10, 19, 20, 24, and 27 February; 1, 15, 18, 20, 23, 25, and 27 March; 11 April; 2 and 6 May; 7, 8, 22, and 28 June; 7, 11, and 22 July; 3, 4, 13, 14, 17, 18, 19, 20, and 30 August; 4, 5, 6, 9, 19, 20, and 30 September; 28 October; 14, 21 December.

Swami Vivekananda, *The Complete Works of Swami Vivekananda,* Vol. III and Vol. IX. Calcutta, © Advaita Ashrama, 1989: 7, 8, 11, and 14 January; 3, 4, 5, 18, 25, and 26 February; 2, 4, 6, 7, 10, 11, and 17 March; 4, 8, 15, 18, 21, 22, 23, 24, 26, and 27 April; 8, 16, and 17 May; 17 and 30 June; 2 and 23 July; 2, 4, 15, 16, 21, 22, 24, 26, and 28 August; 8, 24, 27, 28, and 29 September; 9 and 22 October; 13, 15, 16, 22, 29, and 30 November; 5, 8, 9, 13, 18, 22, and 23 December.

Following *Offerings: Buddhist Wisdom for Every Day*,
Wisdom: 365 Thoughts from Indian Masters is the second volume
in the collection *Offrandes de l'Humanité*, which, every year
in autumn, promotes with a new book the heritage of the great thoughts of one culture.

To learn more about these books: **www.follmi.com**

All photographs of this work were taken by Olivier Föllmi and are available
from the agency RAPHO in Paris **(www.rapho.com).**

Library of Congress Cataloging-in-Publication Data is on file with the Library of Congress.
ISBN: 0-8109-5620-9

© 2001 Éditions de La Martinière, Paris/Éditions Föllmi, Annecy (France)
English translation © 2004 Harry N. Abrams, Inc., and Thames & Hudson, Ltd, London.
Published in 2004 by Harry N. Abrams, Incorporated, New York.
All rights reserved. No part of the contents of this book may be reproduced without written permission of the publisher.

Printed and bound in Italy

10 9 8 7 6 5 4 3 2 1

Harry N. Abrams, Inc.
100 Fifth Avenue
New York, N.Y. 10011
www.abramsbooks.com

Abrams is a subsidiary of

LA MARTINIÈRE
GROUPE

When a man

battles within his soul,